RAINBOW POWER

"Let me, O let me bathe my soul in colors; let me swallow the sunset and drink the rainbow."

KAHLIL GIBRAN

RAIN BOW POWER

✦

Manifest Your Dream Life with the Creative Magic of Color

✦

Jerico Mandybur

BOOKS

Contents

Dream in Color:
an Introduction   6

The Magic of Science   16

A Brief History of   24
Color & Magic

Arranging the Rainbow   34

Tapping into YOUR   42
Rainbow Power

Red   60

Orange   68

Yellow   76

Green   84

Blue   92

Purple   100

Pink   108

Brown   116

Black   124

White   132

Gray   140

Fear No Colors   148

Table of   150
Correspondences

References   152

Acknowledgments   156

About the Author   158

Dream in Color: an Introduction

"Be thou the rainbow to the storms of life, the evening beam that smiles the clouds away, and tints tomorrow with prophetic ray!"

LORD BYRON

The book you have in your hands is about the art of rainbow magic (traditionally called color magic). You will learn how to wield this magic powerfully, whether you're a baby witch, a modern mystic, an emerging artist, or none of the above. This book is *for you* if you want to better access your intuition and creativity, so you can manifest your most colorful, confident, and magical dream life.

Rainbow Power was written to help you reclaim the joy and metaphysical power of color in a world that would sooner see us think and act in only black and white. A world that praises the uniform and the bland, and where too often the colorful among us are chastised and delegitimised.

Color is threatening to this worldview because color is *magic*. Since the birth of humankind, color has been celebrated and revered as a messenger of the Gods.

While the last few hundred years have seen the colors of the rainbow studied as a scientific phenomenon, a potential healing tool, or even a means of emotional manipulation, humans have been expressing the spiritual through colored art for tens of thousands of years. Think: the 14,000-year-old Altamira cave paintings in Spain or First Nations rock art in pre-Australia that dates back at least 50,000 years.

As a tarot-reading witch and creativity coach, I sometimes meet women and nonbinary people who at first become emotionally paralysed in the face of color. Whether in their creative work, personal expression, or spiritual practice, they're not used to simply *playing*. Instead they're plagued by perfectionism, and by "less is more". They haven't allowed themselves to move past predetermined biases such as "I'm not creative" or "I can't wear orange". They've been taught (as we all have in the supposedly-secular world) to take the power of color for granted. To rarely stop to dwell on its power and mystery. When really, playing with color is *the* magical act; it's simple, fun, innate to our species, and requires zero prior experience or a detailed set of supplies.

I've also lived the experience of these clients. In my young adult life, I saw myself foremost as a depressed intellectual, so I dressed accordingly. I largely eschewed ROYGBIV (an acronym for the traditional colors of the rainbow—red, orange, yellow, green, blue, indigo, and violet) aesthetically as well as spiritually, until one of my teachers, astrologer and tarot practitioner Jeff Hinshaw, properly introduced me to the chakra system (see p.39). While the seven main chakras and their associated colors are taught in the West through a framework haphazardly plucked from Eastern religion, they are a prime, but far from sole, example of how our esoteric understanding of color can and does affect our minds, bodies, and lives.

I've long gotten over my aversion to colors. Since then, in my life and my client's lives, I've observed the profound impact that allowing oneself to get imaginative with color yields. Truly magical results. As Wiccan and author Margot Adler describes it, magic is just a "convenient word for a whole set of techniques of the mind. We might conceive of these techniques as including the mobilization of confidence, will, and emotion... the use of imaginative faculties... to achieve necessary ends."

This book covers the science of how colors work, their esoteric history, their psychological effects, cultural associations, and each of their magical meanings and applications, alongside rituals or spells you can perform anytime. But far from offering universal, unchangeable color associations or imposing rules, in *Rainbow Power* I seek to provide inspiration. Your individual and highly-subjective approach to color is yours alone. And it is more powerful than you know.

Each of us has a personal relationship to color. For example, yellow in rainbow magic stands for joy and optimism, but as someone who navigated a traumatic upbringing from within the four mustard-yellow walls of my childhood bedroom, too much yellow can feel stressful and suffocating. While I encourage you to meet yourself at the expanding edges of your associations with certain shades, stretching and reframing how you see the ones you "don't like", my primary aim is nothing less than your liberation. *You're* the main character in this film and you get to choose your own adventure every step of the way.

Rainbow magic is syncretist and anarchic in nature, meaning it respectfully combines many beliefs and follows no particular method or hierarchy. As a solitary witch my influences are eclectic, including eco-feminist traditions. I have a strong belief that our consciousness and emotional state are our greatest tools in magic and manifestation. Or as the 20th century mystic Neville once put it, "imagination is seeing with the eye of God". I encourage you to view this book through all of these perspectives, blended and filtered through your own. In doing so, *Rainbow Power* will offer you new ways of seeing and relating to color. Ways that are reverent, experimental, creative, and highly magical.

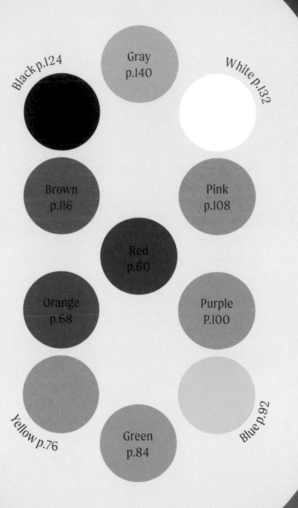

Black p.124

Gray p.140

White p.132

Brown p.116

Pink p.108

Red p.60

Orange p.68

Purple P.100

Yellow p.76

Green p.84

Blue p.92

Rainbow Power presents a unique set of correspondences—a system of symbolic connections, linking one thing to another. In this book, these correspondences are based on the 11 major color groups described in the English language; red, orange, yellow, green, blue, purple, pink, brown, black, white, and gray. Readers familiar with correspondences in formal lineages of magic will see their influence. However, this book is for the rule breakers, and for those keen to take what resonates for them and overlook what doesn't.

Read this book chronologically for a holistic view of the power of color: what it actually is, how it has been interpreted across time, and how each and every color can bring wonder and enjoyment into your life. Then dog-ear your favorite rituals, adjust them to your unique needs, and start making some magic.

Wouldst thou like to live colorfully?

"Living colorfully" is shorthand for embracing your own rainbow power as a tool to affect inner and outer change and create personal transformation in all areas of your life—from self-love and self-care, to your home life, to work, to relationships and dating, and in your spiritual practice. We'll cover them all.

Choosing to live colorfully means you're choosing to step into confidence, find your personal expression, and own your full power as a creative, infinitely magical witch. Because let's admit it, everyday we're up against a lifetime of programming that sees the troll inside our head tell us blatant lies to keep us from our own true worth and luminosity. It says: *you're too much, stop being so cringe, play small, blend in, stay inside the lines.* Worst of all, it echoes the culturally-ascribed feminization (thus invalidation) of all things magical.

Because, as I'm sure you've noticed, the wider world doesn't always appreciate witches. They're the antithesis of everything our modern Western culture worships; rationalism, materialism, and capitalism. So of course your head-troll is trying to keep you from associating with what's so often belittled and delegitimized. Of course it wants to keep you playing small. But you weren't made to play small, were you? You were made magical, color-craving, and capable of joyfully and intuitively expressing your innate worth.

That's why living colorfully is a radical act of individual revolution. It stands for existing at full saturation. It means turning up the brightness and playing in the contrasts. It requires deliberate joy and defiant imagination. To become a color witch is to delve into a process of self-discovery, authenticity, and creativity. In this movie you're the alchemist of your own life; blending and synthesizing colors according to your intended behaviors, outcomes, and deepest, most audacious desires.

Living colorfully isn't about dressing like a kooky art teacher at Pride, or becoming superstitious about all the colors around you. It's simply the intentional and unapologetic application of color through the eyes of a mystic. That's how we've used color for many, many millennia. It's time to get reacquainted with our own magic.

Accessing and owning your rainbow power will allow you to better transform how you feel, how you see yourself, and the whole world you inhabit. It will help you to spark your imagination, increase your pleasure, and create your dream life. It will aid you in becoming more self-assured, fully expressed, and connected to the energetic, magical frequencies all around and within you. Are you ready to color your world? Let's ride this rainbow.

The
Magic
of
Science

> *"Philosophy will clip an Angel's wings,*
> *Conquer all mysteries by rule and line,*
> *Empty the haunted air, the gnomed mine—*
> *Unweave a rainbow"*

JOHN KEATS

Color is fundamental to our process of making meaning in the world. Without it, we wouldn't know which animals are poisonous, which fruit is ripe, or how to interpret traffic signs. But the thing about color is that it doesn't actually exist. Is your mind blown? It should be. Rather than being a concrete type of matter, color is what happens when our mind interprets the vibrations dancing in front of our eyes.

Everything in the universe vibrates. It's our senses that convert this cosmic flurry of electromagnetic waves into concepts like smells, tastes, and colors. Our feeble human eyes can only detect a fraction of this vast field of waves. What we call "color" is the relatively small spectrum of visible light wedged right in the middle of that wider field, which also contains gamma rays, X-rays, ultraviolet light, infrared, and radio waves.

When we view all possibilities of visible light at once, our brains translate it to "white". When we view an object like a red apple, we're witnessing a wavelength of roughly 0.0007 millimeters, where all colors except red are present. We see a red apple because it contains every color *but* red. Red is the wavelength being "rejected" and thus reflected outward. How ironic that we celebrate the color of objects, when the very color we admire is absent.

When light shines on a crystal or a dress or the leaf on a tree, it rearranges its electrons. Some light is absorbed and some—the kind that doesn't match its natural vibration—is reflected back out as color. When light hits our eye, it passes through to the retina, within which live millions of light-sensitive cells called rods and cones. These help us to tell the difference between light and dark, and to read color, respectively.

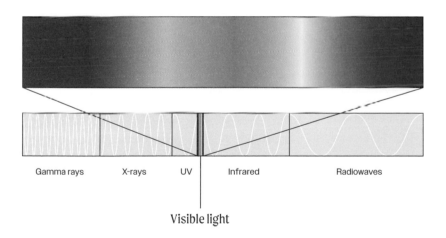

| Gamma rays | X-rays | UV | Infrared | Radiowaves |

Visible light

Unweaving Rainbows

Confusion arises in understanding how color works because there are two kinds of color mixing that yield two very different results: additive and subtractive mixing. Blending all variations of colored light creates white. This is additive mixing. Meanwhile—as most of us find out in early childhood art class—combining every variation of colored paint together creates black. This is subtractive mixing. The more pigments added, the more colors are reflected outward, resulting in our eye interpreting a black-ish brown mess of paint where we assumed a rainbow would be.

As for rainbows themselves? They're what happens when light bounces off drops of rain, becoming refracted into separate wavelengths. This process was emulated by a 24-year-old Sir Isaac Newton in 1666 when he shone white light through a glass prism and a rainbow was projected onto the wall of his dark room. He then passed the rainbow light through a second upside-down prism, and found the colors blended into white again.

It took Newton 8 years to publish his findings but when he did, he categorized the color he saw into seven bands: red, orange, yellow, green, blue, indigo, and violet (or ROYGBIV). Why these seven? Why the addition of indigo (or dark blue) when it's not actually visible in a rainbow? Because Newton was a sucker for symbolic correspondences himself. In the Western world, there were seven musical notes, seven known planets, and seven days of the week. He added indigo with the intention to align color, music, and astronomy. The Romantic poet John Keats would later write that in his work, Newton had "destroyed all the poetry of the rainbow by reducing it to prismatic colors".

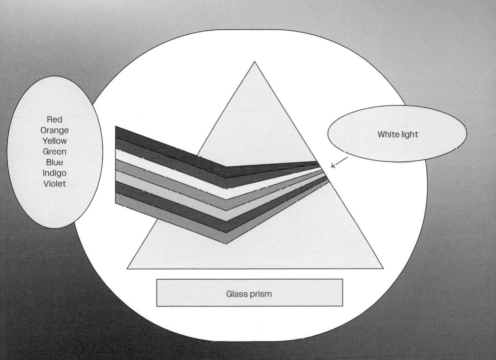

Red
Orange
Yellow
Green
Blue
Indigo
Violet

White light

Glass prism

Beyond Science

Scientifically speaking, we know that color has helped life on earth evolve. It offers camouflage, it can attract, and it can offer a warning as a form of self-protection. In humans, it affects our bodies and our minds too. When light strikes the cone cells of our eyes, it sends messages to the brain and specifically the hypothalamus. In concert with our pituitary gland, the hypothalamus governs body temperature, appetite, sleep, sexual functions, metabolism, the nervous system, and their associated psychological reactions.

Makes sense, right? We've all experienced our mood lift in the warm glow of the sun, or felt a little numb inside an all-gray cubicle. Color directly affects our physical selves, our emotional response, wellbeing, and our experience of the world. And while we all have that in common, the use of rainbow power is an individual journey. Literally. Because each of us sees color differently. There's no way we can ever know if what you call "green" and what I call "green" are the same thing. Neither of us are right or wrong—color is just physiologically unique as well as emotionally subjective.

Think of the 4% of the population who have color vision issues a.k.a color blindness. Is their understanding of color more or less correct than someone else's? What about people with tetrachromacy, the condition that sees them born with four channels of cones, instead of three, giving them the ability to recognise 10,000 more hues than the average person. Should we hold their interpretation of color as the correct one? What about people with synesthesia who associate colors with letters, days of the week, or musical notes?

As you can see, while color can be studied as a scientific phenomenon, it's anything but homogenous. Rather, it's an enigma. A mystery. An illusion. And that's exactly why the history of color theory cannot be separated from the history of magic.

A Brief History of Color & Magic

"Color is a power which directly influences the soul."

WASSILY KANDINSKY

Throughout time, alchemists, philosophers, and mystics have attempted to understand the nature of color and its seemingly divine impact on the mind, body, emotions, and on the invisible energetic plane of the magical. In their workings, the frequencies of color were used (and still are by some) in a spiritual manner to produce healing, metaphysical change, and real-world effects. Not least of these is all the joy and play that fills one's life when we choose to live colorfully.

There is not *one* history of rainbow magic. In all corners of the world, color has jumped the hedge between secular and sacred. In every context, color's symbolism, cultural associations, and uses have varied, often carrying multiple meanings at one time. As a multicultural member of the modern Western world, the following brief history of color represents a culture I'm part of. I encourage you to create your own.

400s BCE

Plato thought of colors as luminous "effluences" or flames. He understood color as a kind of light that existed independently from the objects it shone through.

300s BCE

Aristotle taught that colors were rays of celestial light. Believing that all colors sprang from light or the lack of it, he saw black and white as the only primary colors. He also created a system of correspondences where certain colors stood for times of the day, with white at midday and black at midnight.

250s CE

In Plotinus' *The Enneads*, color belongs to the realm of essence, rather than physical form; a spiritual idea that anthropologist Amy Hale notes has similarities with the modern abstract art movement of the 20th century, which was seen as a liberation from form.

900–107

Physician Abu 'Ali al-Husayn ibn Sina (or Avicenna) taught that color could be used to diagnose and cure illnesses. He noticed that, like plants, sick people lose color and that red light stimulates the movement of blood, while blue light soothes. He thus made in-roads in the use of color as a healing aid.

1500s

Alchemist Paracelsus' mission was to lead doctors back to the divine, believing the Sun ruled the heart of human beings, the Moon ruled the brain, and so on. In his work, color and light (along with music, herbs, and talismans) were vital in the treatment of disease and disharmony.

1533

Occultist Cornelius Agrippa's *Three Books of Occult Philosophy* presents colors as corresponding to planets, zodiac signs, and elements, writing "colors contain the influence of the stars to which they have sympathetic qualities." He influenced the Hermetic systems used by 19th century magicians, which in turn impact witches today. His system appropriated heavily from Jewish mysticism, called Kabbalah.

1810

Polymath Goethe's poetic theories of color were a refutation of Newton's. While scientifically rejected, they were embraced in the field of color theory, particularly the impact color can have on one's psychology and emotional state. Goethe's theories were furthered by painter Phillip Otto Runge. Runge's work was a huge influence (along with appropriated Eastern spirituality) on the creation of Theosophy— the hugely influential religion that all modern witchcraft owes a debt to.

1890s

The influential Hermetic Order of the Golden Dawn relished the invention of new pigments and color knowledge. As a scientifically-friendly occult order, they developed the use of color magic in complex and layered ways that complemented their Hermetic interpretation of the Tree of Life: a system for understanding divinity in Jewish Kabbalah (spelled Qabalah by Hermetcists).

1929

Psychoanalyst Carl Jung is inspired by the writing of the ancient Greek physician Hippocrates to create four personality types based on four colors, in an effort to categorize and better explain human behavior. His colors were cool blue, earth green, sunshine yellow, and fiery red.

1959

Philosopher Rudolf Steiner saw each color as a living entity with its own spiritual significance. He believed it had untapped potential in medicine and that art could help humans reconnect with their higher selves.

1971

Professor Max Luscher posits that both physical and psychological illnesses can be treated with color, basing his belief on the theory that a person's preferences for certain colors are based on the "emotional value" of those colors and indicative of personality traits.

1970s

Enter chaos magic. Rather than a system in which people ascend in occult knowledge and power based on experience, as ceremonial orders required, here was one where each color could be read as a kind of spirit, deity, or egregore (an entity imbued with the collective meaning and strength assigned to it over the course of history). In chaos magic, interpretations and practices are a personal choice.

1992

In the book *Liber Kaos*, chaos magician Peter J. Carroll creates the symbol of the chaos star to represent his theory of the eight forms of magic, based on the eight colors of the Hermetic Qabalah's sephiroth (meaning infinite emanations) on the Tree of Life. The colors of the chaos star are far from static though. They've since been adapted to represent the colors of the Wiccan Sabbats and more.

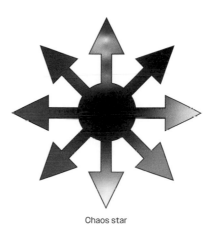

Chaos star

PRESENT

No matter what your belief system, the choices we make regarding our daily interactions with color are ours alone. And that autonomy should be celebrated. However, there's no denying that colors contain symbolic and deeply affecting (if not outright spiritual) resonance, as well as emotional vibrations and even physical reactions—whether we want them to or not. From a witch's perspective, color can and will carry out its own agenda. So we may as well make friends with the rainbow and let it influence those areas of life most precious to us. Right?

A FEAR OF COLOR

Color is expressed through language in vastly different ways. The Russian language has two words for blue. Hindi sees saffron as a major color but has no one standard word to describe gray. In some cultures, blue and green are interchangeable and in others, there are multiple words for shades of the "same" color. In essence, our ways of seeing are unique to culture, context, and the subjective experiences and beliefs of the person seeing them.

Ancient Egyptians had a complex system of color symbolism. Ancient Greek philosophers too, as we've seen, saw color as proof of universal harmony. The ancient Druids of England, according to Éliphas Lévi in *The History of Magic*, carried colorful talismans and herbs because they were said to attract the light of the stars. Meanwhile, early Brahmanism revered yellow as sacred and Buddha too is often associated with yellow or gold.

The Chinese philosopher Confucius who was born in the 6th century BCE, wore black, white, and yellow and wrote about disliking purple "because it confuses us with the red color". Since the birth of Islam, green has been associated with divinity and the eternal paradise they believe awaits us. And in Judaism and Christianity, blue is associated with the heavens and the Virgin Mary respectively.

Human fascination with color is a great mystery. Why, despite our differences, do all cultures designate meaning and magical properties to tricks of light? As color theorist Faber Birren wrote in 1950, in the early history of the world, "nearly all color expression concerned mysticism and the enigmas of life and death". But as the wheel of time spun on—with religious dogma growing, the might of empires spreading, and the industrial revolution booming—ancient and Indigenous reverence for color was replaced by a kind of "chromophobia", as artist David Batchelor calls it. Chromophobia is a white, western, orientalist-inspired collective fear of color that can be seen in art and literature, particularly at the turn of the 20th century.

The purpose of this social narrative was to distinguish one's self from the Other, whose sumptuous and vivid use of color was said to threaten the social order with its garish display of implied desire and debauchery. Since then, Batchelor says, color has been "systematically marginalized, reviled, diminished, and degraded." And the effects of this cultural othering loom large today; minimalism in home decor is coded as classic and chic. Joyful displays of color in the home? They're usually seen as eccentric or exotic. In a film, a white shirt and trousers are read as elegant and timeless, while a hot pink halter top is code for promiscuous or bimbo.

What we might think of as our personal biases regarding color are often entirely by design. That's what makes living colorfully by reclaiming your love of color (whether a little or a lot) and its magical, transformational potential such a badass move.

Arranging the Rainbow

*"Color is the place where our brain
and the universe meet."*

PAUL KLEE

Human beings love systems of categorization. We thrive when grouping things together to create meaning and we're lowkey obsessed with pattern recognition. And for most witches and magical people, it's no different; we love correspondences. And while rainbow magic doesn't emphasize a rigid set of symbolic associations (you're welcome to tweak or discard the table of correspondences at the back of this book), understanding the "this goes with that" of magical correspondences is an amazing opportunity to understand the rules, so you can choose whether or not you break them on your journey to living colorfully.

If magic, as defined by Aleister Crowley, is the "science and art of causing change to occur in conformity with one's will", then what's called sympathetic magic is the use of concepts, objects, or actions that resemble or symbolize that which you'd like to cause change to or influence. Rainbow magic (and any magic that utilizes correspondences) falls under the umbrella of sympathetic magic.

For example, in creating an altar to the Sun, a color witch might gather sunflowers, gold or yellow candles, The Sun tarot card, and a glyph signifying the zodiac sign of Leo. This is because all these things correspond to the Sun in magic. In other words, they're correspondences.

The majority of these correspondences were created by during the Hermetic revival of the Renaissance and, even more so, by occultists of the last two centuries with a renewed interest in this revival. These magicians were the first to fuse (or more accurately, culturally appropriate) Eastern spiritual concepts into their framework of correspondences. The New Age movement of the '70s and '80s took this even further. Now, finding the correspondences between crystals, yoga asanas, zodiac signs, and any other category you can think of is just one Google away.

For the purposes of this book, I've created some brief explainers to honor a few key spiritual systems that correspond closely with common forms of color magic. I share these not as an expert but as an invitation: if these systems light you up, spark your imagination, or fill you with a sense of magical conviction, that's amazing! Find the texts and teachers firmly centered within these traditions and practice their teachings responsibly.

THE CHAKRA SYSTEM

Chakra (cha-kruh) is a Sanskrit word meaning wheel, disc, or any circular arrangement. As tantric scholar Harish Johari puts it, chakras are "psychic centers of transformation that enable one to move toward an enlightened state of being." They can't be described materially because they don't belong to the material body; rather they're a part of the "subtle" body, composed of vital life force (prana) distributed via channels of energy (nadis) which connect the chakras.

The term "chakra" is used in the Yogashikka Upanishad of 100 BC—300 BCE, but it wasn't until the medieval period that the presence of four or more chakras in the subtle body are acknowledged in Hindu and Buddhist texts. Gorakshanath wrote of the "six plus one" major chakras in *Goraksha Śataka*, written somewhere between 900—1400. This inspired the modern belief that there are seven major chakras.

In the West today each chakra is strongly associated with a color of the ROYGBIV rainbow. The Western names for each chakra, in ascending order: root chakra, sacral chakra, solar plexus, heart chakra, throat chakra, third eye, and crown chakra. Within tantra, each chakra has its own set of spiritual correspondences; deities, elements, seed sounds (bija mantras), images (yantras), animals, planets, and so on.

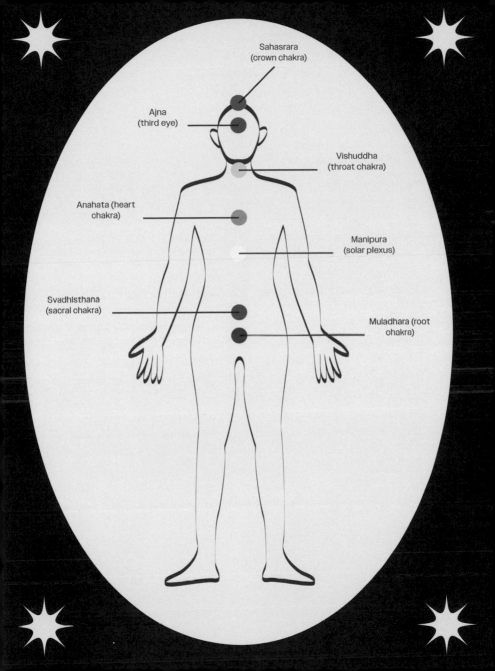

Sahasrara
(crown chakra)

Ajna
(third eye)

Vishuddha
(throat chakra)

Anahata (heart
chakra)

Manipura
(solar plexus)

Svadhisthana
(sacral chakra)

Muladhara (root
ohakra)

AURAS

Auras are usually spoken about as a complement to the chakra system, because they're another representation of a human being's subtle body. Put simply, auras are a rainbow-colored emanation of energy that surrounds our bodies and can be seen by spiritual intuitives. The colors of our aura depict our personality, health, and psychological state in any given moment. And these colors generally correspond with the seven major chakra colors. Much like the popularization of the chakra system in the West, auras as we know them today were a product of Victorian Theosophy.

Theosophist Charles Webster Leadbeater (a former Church of England priest) studied in India, as the founder of Theosophy, Helena Blavatsky, had done. In 1910, he published the highly influential *The Inner Life*, in which he blended the concept of auras and chakras, mixing them with his own ideas. These ideas were again reinterpreted by thinkers like Rudolf Steiner and Edgar Cayce, who in turn inspired the '70s esotericist Christopher Hills. Hills is usually credited with assigning the chakras and auras the ROYGBIV rainbow in a flattened, simple way. And the rest is New Age history.

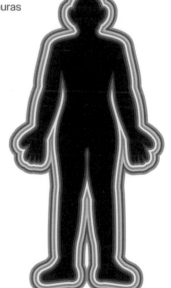

TAROT

Inspired by the Hermetic Order of the Golden Dawn's intricate color correspondences, two members of the Order, Arthur Edward Waite and Pamela Colman Smith, created the most famous and authoritative tarot deck in history, the Rider Waite Smith deck of 1909. Within it lies a world of color symbolism that has been written about ever since.

Most modern tarot decks, to some extent, are influenced in their use of color by Colman Smith's paintings. Some—like the deck I created called *Neo Tarot*, illustrated by Daiana Ruiz—make use of color through their own lens of interpretation. Still, any tarot reader or admirer would be hard pressed to see a card containing lots of red and not think of ardor, strength, or intensity, or one with lots of black and not think of grief or the great unknown. When tarot readers see orange in a card, typically speaking, they might think of passion or enthusiasm, while purple often speaks to opulence or compassion, blue to spirituality or expansion, green for harmony or growth, yellow for curiosity or intellectualism, gray for gloom or objectivity, and white for purity of intention.

Tapping into YOUR Rainbow Power

"Color...thinks by itself, independently of the object it cloaks."

CHARLES BAUDELAIRE

It doesn't take the world to access your unique brand of rainbow power. All it takes is a little imagination. And I mean that literally. There's a saying in the world of chaos magic, "belief as a tool". That means that using your singular and gorgeous values, creative ideas, and imaginative faculties is the key to pure effing magic.

Neville taught that every individual's imagination is divine—a kind of God. As occult historian Mitch Horowitz describes this idea, we live "within an infinite network of coexistent realities, from which we select ... experiences by the nature of our emotionalized thoughts and expectations." Meaning: each of us manifests all we experience through our own mind.

To put it another way, the world around you is formed by you. By your thoughts, feelings, choices, and perceptions of it. As Horowitz says, "you are what you see and you see what you are." Just as quantum theory proposes a world of particles that react to conscious observation, so magic suggests that you can affect the very course of your life through imagination, intention, and action. In other words, by having a magical, meaningful perspective about yourself and the world around you, you can create a life you love.

Does "selecting your reality" or manifesting your dreams imply you're responsible for the world's great tragedies or any injustices that befall you? Absolutely not. In this view, destructive systems of domination could be seen as the antithesis of imagination and creativity; the result of centuries and centuries of empire and industry built on greed and corruption. The result for ordinary people like you and me? Too often believing the lie that we're powerless, cut off from our own imaginative faculties instead of cultivating them.

It's exactly these faculties—these internal sources of vibrancy, energy, hope, and magic—that allow you to reimagine what you're truly capable of doing. And undoing. Color, like belief, is your tool.

How to start living colorfully

If rainbow magic had its own manifesto, the first point would be this: color is *alive*. Like everything around us, it vibrates, dancing and singing at a frequency imperceptible but very much measurable. Magically speaking, you might say color has its own will to exist—to create beauty, cause pleasure, even seek to influence. As artist Wassily Kandinksy once wrote, "Color hides a power still unknown but real, which acts on every part of the human body."

Living colorfully doesn't mean you have to change anything about yourself and your life that you don't already *love*. It's about loving those things even louder and brighter. And anything you need to release (think: the shame of taking up space, the fear of other people's judgment, the last shred of cynicism keeping you from 100% owning your magic) you can let go.

Rainbow power is your permission slip. It will show you the door to living your most powerful, playful, colorful life *and* it will walk you through it. Rather than thinking of living colorfully as an aesthetic—it doesn't matter what you wear or how you look—think of it as a fresh new perspective. Or more accurately, a re-remembering of your original one. A reclaiming of that brave, imaginative, extremely magical little kid you once were.

When I was young, I would pick up rocks along the beach. Finding some particularly intriguing, I would deem them "masters". Not all rocks were masters, but the ones that were, they had a power and a wisdom not of this world. They would whisper magical secrets to only those who could recognize their true nature. My sister and dad would laugh: "that's just a wet rock!" But I saw beyond appearances. Beyond the labels of everyday mundane "things". This is what rainbow power requires of us—to remember our *awe*. To embrace the spirit and the potent, proven effect of colors, so that we can make use of them mindfully. And take them for granted no more.

The rituals that follow will allow you to reframe your relationship with color and stretch your intuitive abilities in new ways. If you're new to divination, great! Enjoy experimenting and journaling your results. And if you feel a little silly while doing this? Amazing. You're allowed to be silly *and* spiritual. In *Neo Tarot* I said "there are no tarot police" and the same is true for your rainbow power. The way that works for you is *the* way.

Psychic daydreaming

"Daydreaming subverts the world."

RAOUL VANEIGEM

Rather than thinking of color as its own benevolent consciousness, it's helpful to think of it as a loving but rather neutral expansive force. It collaborates with us, amplifying the potential of the energy that's already there. For example, have you ever noticed how much more confident you feel with a red lip? Or how untouchable black sunglasses make you feel? That's because color can lead us towards the aligned expression of who we really are. It invites the dormant qualities—of ourselves and of the energy vibing all around us—out to play.

"Play" is the operative word. If you're new to witchcraft and living a little more magically, the practice of play might feel foreign. And fair enough. Suspending disbelief may not come overnight if you've spent your whole life taking color for granted. But the path of wielding your rainbow power isn't stern and formal. It's a path of deliberate, defiant irreverence.

So *how* do you begin using your imagination as a tool of manifestation in magic? Start with a visualization practice that mystics, evidence-based psychologists, scientists, and new-agers alike all have a version of. I call it psychic daydreaming.

HOW TO PSYCHICALLY DAYDREAM:

- First, get crystal clear on what you most want emotionally. Not the external outcome that you think will bring you validation, stability, or envy. The desire *behind* the desire. What gives you the fullest sense of meaning, purpose, deep fulfillment, or joy? *That* thing. And what's the most ethical method of inviting it in? Yeah, that.

- Sit or lie down with your eyes closed or your gaze soft. Imagine attaining your desired state, bathed in the colors you most associate with this state. The emotional foreplay is what makes this practice magnetic. Visualize the state as if it is happening *right now*. Play out the scene in real time; the way you feel, the actions you take, the effect they have, the satisfying fulfillment of all that you'd wished for.

- Importantly, sense the embodied feelings throughout, as if you're fully inhabiting the body of your future self. *Feel* it all on an emotional and physical level. Because the feeling is the magic. Colorful imagery just acts as an imaginative aid to encourage a kind of mindlessness. Daydream like this until you sense a feeling of completion.

Daydream as part of your spells or rituals, whether you use the ones in this book or invent your own as part of your daily/weekly manifestation practice.

Cleansing and charging colors

Before using a color in a spell, ritual, or in everyday life, I recommend that witches cleanse/bless it. This removes any preexisting energies and freshens them up for use. But it doesn't have to involve a lot of rigmarole. You can simply cleanse the colored object/s with smoke from ethically sourced herbs or incense. You could also use salt water, sound (singing, clapping, or using instruments like a bell or drum) or by taking a few seconds to cleanse with intention, mentally.

Charging a color or object is about magically programming it. When you charge something, you imbue it with the full power of your intention. Hold the object against your heart, then whisper your desired outcome to it. Or gaze at the color softly, while taking deep purposeful breaths and holding your focus on your desired outcome. You can put your colored objects in the sunlight or moonlight to soak them with the magic of the most useful celestial body. Or again, you could utilize sound.

This is not an exhaustive list. Charge colors in a way that sparks your unique imagination and suits your objective. And if you aren't using a particular colored object (for example, if you're petitioning a certain color to appear more frequently in your reality) remember you can always close your eyes, put on a song that reminds you of that color, and commune with it virtually. And if you need a little outside stimulation, just find a picture of the color and look at it. There's a world of meditative artwork, wallpapers, and virtual posters to help you.

As always, the most effective form of magic is the one you have on hand. Belief is your tool. If you don't yet believe? Act as if you do and see what happens! You might just surprise yourself.

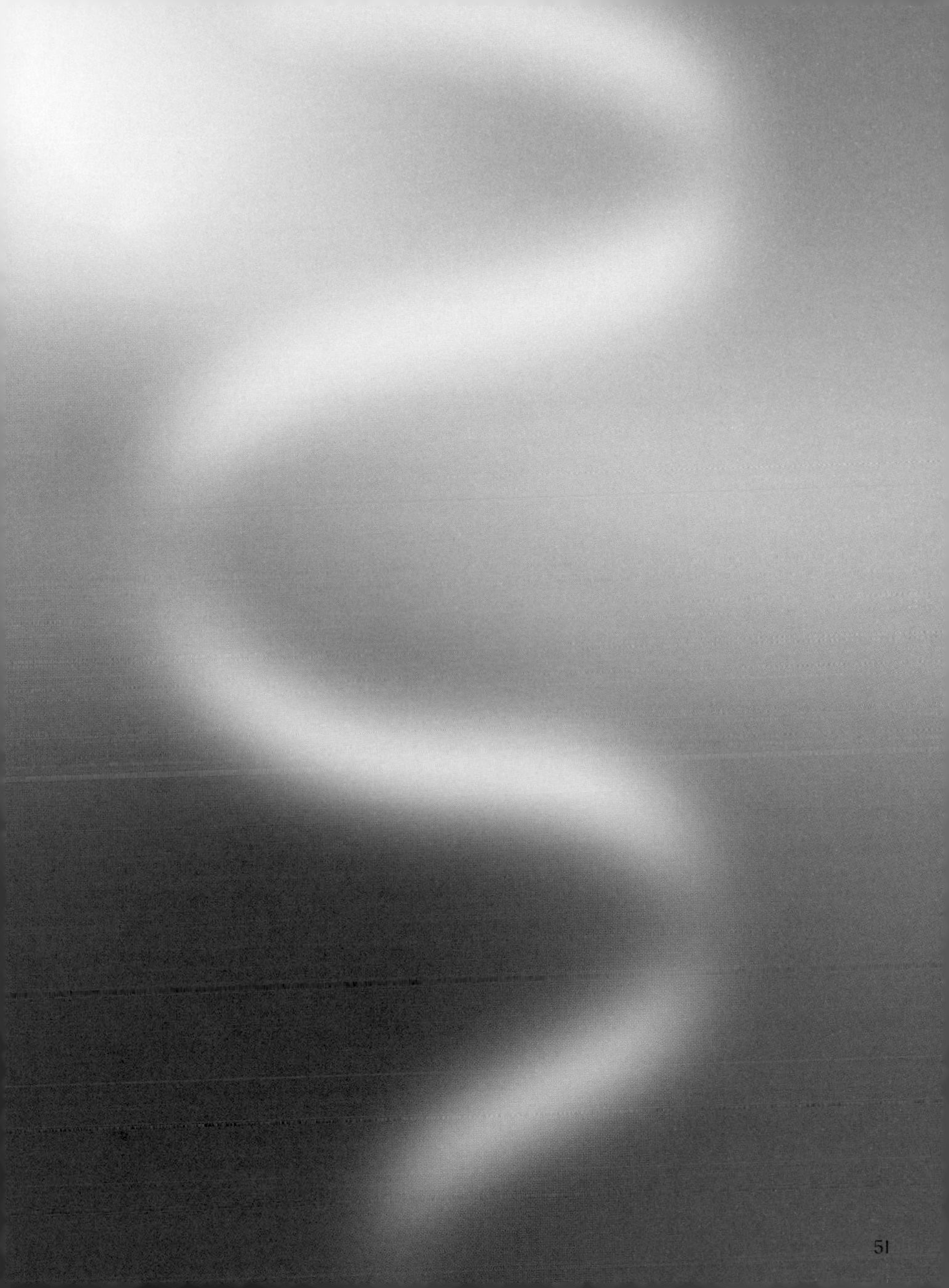

Your color personality

What rainbow of colors best represents you, heart and soul? What unique palette do you use to paint your life? I'm not going to ask you to do a personality test to assign you only one color. That would be a cop-out. Instead, I want you to pick up a pen and a journal and do the creative ritual on the facing page, adapted from one of my teachers, Jill Badonsky, an author and the founder of Kaizen Muse creativity coaching.

Close your eyes if that feels good. And just breathe. Feel the aliveness of your body. Bring to mind all the joy and freedom you feel when doing what you love most. Allow a slight smile to appear on your face. Once you're in a relaxed, meditative state, answer the following questions—allowing yourself to quickly write down whatever associations and words first come to mind, without censorship.

If my unique magic was a noise, it would sound like...

If it were a dance move, it would be...

My magic smells like...

My magic tastes like...

If it was a bumper sticker, it would say...

If it was an animal, my magic would be...

The texture of my magic is...

If it was an item of clothing my magic would be...

If my magic was a flower, it would be...

If it was screaming, my magic would shout...

If my magic was to whisper, it would say...

If my magic was a color, it would be...

If my magic was feeling goofy it would...

If it were feeling powerful and fierce it would...

The wind in trees

Exaggerated shimmies

Freshly cut grass

Strawberry soy-shakes

Stay soft

A green tree frog

Fluffy cashmere

A sequin onesie

Purple orchids

I am alive!

You are safe

Ocean blue, deep green, gold, and purple

Belch loudly

Howl at the moon

Now that you've completed the ritual, here comes the rad part. Take all the answers to your prompts and again, without censorship, string them together to form an absurd yet beautifully descriptive, sacred poem. Now read it aloud to yourself. What feelings does your poem inspire in you? What new insights can you draw from it? Any recurring themes? Color schemes?

This ritual can show you what colors (and their associated characteristics) you may want to seek out more of. For example, if lots of cool colors like greens and blues emerged, look up the attributes and correspondences of the "warm" colors in this book, like red and orange to see if you'd like to incorporate a little more of them into your magical practice and life. It's all about balance. And it's your call.

Bonus points if you go on to journal about your color preferences: why are you drawn to the colors you're drawn to? What memories do you associate with your go-to colors? How do they make you feel? What emotions do you associate those colors with?

You get a gold star if you use the above questions to do some emotional unpacking around the colors you *don't* currently like too! There's some gems to be dug up there. It might even be the start of a newly reframed relationship with your least favorite colors. Go on, give 'em a chance.

Color dowsing

Whether you're a beginner to woo woo, or an experienced witch, sparking your intuitive faculties when it comes to color is a world unto itself. Color dowsing is a simply intuitive ritual that anyone can do with a little imagination, creativity, and self-trust. The purpose of this ritual? To get some insight into what color you need more of in your life. This could be your emotional life, your physical health, your magical workings, or all of the above. The specifics are up to you, but the goal is the same: to receive an intuitive message from the color whose energies could serve you well in this moment. Think of it as a personal color prescription.

HOW TO COLOR DOWSE:

- Take a crystal pendulum. If you don't have one you can use a cleansed ring on a necklace chain, or a sewing needle, safety pin, shell, pendant, or button threaded with string. Now breathe deeply and allow yourself to enter a relaxed, open state. Once you're ready, ask your pendulum (out loud or in your mind's eye) to show you the color you're most in need of.

- Hold the chain or string directly in the middle of the color wheel opposite, with your hand still. Soon, your pendulum will swing in a certain direction, typically over two colors opposite each other on the wheel. One color will have slightly more force behind it. That is your prescribed color. The other is your complimentary—use it in small doses to balance out the effects of the dominant one.

- If you're unsure which of the two colors is more dominant, draw a "yes" and a "no" box next to the wheel or on a separate piece of paper and ask a closed question (e.g. "Is pink my dominant color in this reading?") to clarify.

Learn all about your prescribed color (and complementary one) in its individual chapter and put it to work. It's clearly got some emotional and spiritual lessons it wants to share with you!

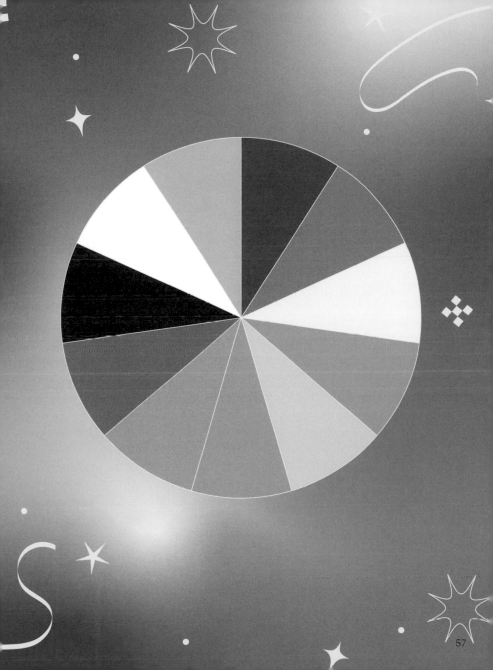

Ribbon reading

Ribbon reading is a form of divination that came to prominence during the turn of the last century, when Spiritualist practices (like mediumship and seances) were huge, as was wearing ribbons in one's hair. Flex your intuition as well as your color interpretation muscles by giving yourself a ribbon reading and using the color chapters in this book for reference.

HOW TO DO A RIBBON READING:

- First, procure ribbons in every color. Once you've got them, find a quiet space and place them in front of you in a pile. Breathe and allow yourself to enter a meditative state.

- When you're ready, ask a question, similar to what you might ask in a tarot reading. To start, try asking "where is my energy at right now?", or "what do I need to know about _____ right now?"

- With your eyes closed, pick up one piece of ribbon. Without looking at it, check in with your senses. Contemplate what that color *feels* like: what words come to mind? Open your eyes and see what color has answered your question. Is it the color you expected? How might it relate to the question you asked?

- Refer to this book's color meanings and consider how they relate to your situation. Journal your interpretations (trying using colored markers) and revisit them often to see what themes emerge.

Congrats! You've formed your very own interpretations of colors and their magic. Ribbon reading is also a really fun and easy ritual to do with friends.

Getting creative

These are just a few examples of rituals and exercises you can do as a witch devoted to living colorfully. Truthfully, in using your rainbow power there is nothing—no activity or creative process—that is not a spell. Anything and everything you do involving color, with the right intention, can be a magical act. How radically freeing is that? From now on, anytime you interact with or even think about color, you can turn it into a DIY ritual.

That means using a coloring book, wearing a mood ring, going to that yoga class (you know, the one that's inclusive and doesn't water down the teachings of Hinduism), thrifting by color, taking a photo of your energy with an aura camera, wearing certain colors to attain a certain meditative state of mind, playing with tie-dye or food coloring, wearing drugstore makeup in wild hues, eating foods in the colors you love, inventing your own colorful visualizations, writing affirmations using a rainbow of gel pens, and literally anything else you can think of.

The following chapters will offer you color-specific rituals to get you started. Promise me you'll make them your own. I want you to use them to show up big and live out loud. In full color.

Red

"When in doubt, wear red."

BILL BLASS

USES IN MAGIC

Power, courage, desire, strength, action, attraction

IN AN AURA

Passion, vitality, change, anger, pioneering

PLANET

Mars

ZODIAC

Aries

DAY OF THE WEEK

Tuesday

ELEMENT

Fire

DIRECTION

South in the Northern Hemisphere, North in the Southern Hemisphere

CHAKRA

Muladhara (meaning "base")

TAROT CARD

The Emperor, The Tower

CRYSTALS

Garnet, red jasper, ruby

HERBS

Dandelion root, ginger, ashwagandha

FOODS

Radishes, beets (beetroots), red onions, tomatoes, turnip, chilies, strawberries, paprika

HEALING QUALITIES

Boosts heart rate, adrenaline, circulation, increases heat

PSYCHOLOGICAL ASSOCIATIONS

Grabbing attention, irritation, urgency, impulsivity, lust, temper, blood, dignity, dominance

The source of red pigment for most of human history, including today, is blood. Yes, some of your favorite red lipsticks are made with insect blood from cochineal or carmine bugs. Incan and Aztec society valued rich cochineal reds as God-attracting shades. In Ancient Egypt, bodies were usually wrapped in red derived from the iron ore hematite, in preparation for the soul's encounter with Osiris, who the *Book of the Dead* calls "Lord of the red cloth".

Naturally, red has also been associated closely with power. Cochineal red was reserved for Roman generals. Armies across time have worn red, despite being a terrible color to camouflage. Red is the most common color in national flags, and the color is still associated with the ruling class, whether the red-cloaked cardinals of the Vatican or the red carpet of movie premieres. Red's other great association? Lust and transgression. Think: red-light districts, the whore of Babylon riding a "scarlet-colored beast" in the Bible's Revelations, and the Scarlet Woman herself, the Goddess (also called Babalon) of Aleister Crowley's Thelemic tradition, who represents liberated feminine desire.

This dynamic blend of power and lust makes red a potent force in the minds and hearts of its observers. And in rainbow magic, that potency becomes a way to cause all kinds of positive change.

RED AT HOME

Red's primary effect is a physical one—it's said to increase adrenaline. But don't be afraid! Magically utilizing red in your home (like any color) just requires thoughtful intention. Rainbow magic is not just about creating a mood. It's the act of cultivating certain kinds of action that lead to an intended result. And red is *the* perfect color to embolden action.

Think of red as the helpful fire under your butt—pushing you to be brave and do the damn thing. Want more motivation to eat properly? Put red magnets on your refrigerator to fire up your appetite. Want to get up earlier? Buy a red alarm clock to boost your stamina. Need more motivation when working from home? Put a red sticker on your laptop.

If you're looking to better embody your sexual power, your home will love red. Let it inspire your passion by seeing—and using—red as a seductive force in your living space. Whether you live alone or with others, red is capable of kickstarting your erotic self-worth by reminding you of your true nature as a desiring, desired being who's totally deserving of sensual satisfaction. Place blood-red roses on your bed stand, sleep in slinky red sleepwear, and indulge in a lush red bath bomb until you feel the deep truth of your sexiness soaking in.

RED IN CLOTHING + BEAUTY

At the 2004 Olympics games, combat athletes who wore red won 55% of the time. While no one knows why phenomena like this occur, it seems red triggers the flight part of "fight or flight" in observers. Which means it's a witch's job to use it responsibly.

Studies have shown wearing red increases one's allure too; wait staff are tipped more when wearing red and women are subconsciously seen as more desirable. Such is the promise of forbidden pleasure that red delivers. Red is always noticed first. That implies dominance or even defiance, depending on the context. But either way, it's laudable and looked up to.

Put on some fierce red sneakers or laces when you want to harness the motivation you need to go for a run. Throw on a bright red outfit when you're really feeling yourself—and watch how many heads you turn. Hell, dye your hair red and feel the power seep in through every strand. Paint your nails red to inspire a "hands on" approach when asserting yourself, such as sending a semi-scary email. Wear red lipstick like a warpaint when you need to find *just* the right words in a negotiation. This is the craft of witches' glamour in action.

RED AT WORK

When it comes to dressing for work using your rainbow power, it's all about knowing how you want to feel and behave—and because this is work—how you want *others* to feel too. Red is a color of leadership, energy, drive, and self-assurance. Wear it when you'd like to be seen as an employee of conviction, a formidable office opponent, when you have a physically demanding day ahead of you, or when you want to impress everyone at your next presentation. Try keeping a red crystal or pomodoro (tomato timer) on your desk to stay in your power with your eyes firmly on the prize—whatever that looks like for you.

PSA: An excess of red in the home or workplace, like red walls, can sometimes bring out tense emotions like frustration or anger in sensitive or easily-overheated individuals. Experiment to find the right balance of reds for you.

RITUAL: LIGHT YOUR FIRE

This simple spell is designed to help you embody
and embrace your full power as a creature of desire,
drawing that which lights your fire closer to you.

First, light a red candle (in a fire-safe holder or dish free from
obstruction) in a quiet, cleansed space decorated with
things—including red ones—that remind you of your power. If
those qualities feel far away from you right now, use the wonder
of your imagination. Ask yourself, what if the objects in front of
me filled me with more awareness of my own power? What
could it feel like to draw upon my deepest sense of deserving?

Take some nourishing deep breaths and feel your breath flowing
all the way down to the base of your spine, soaking up strength
with each inhale. Breathe out a rich red mist of power that
surrounds you with each exhale.

Take a red pen or marker and some paper. While continuing to
breathe energizing red, ask yourself "what lights my fire?" Make
a stream of consciousness list of your turn ons, your most
thrilling sensations, wildest dreams, passions, and brazen
desires. List them as unapologetically and without censorship
as you are able. See the red ink emanating that same mist and
bask in the excitement that is claiming what's yours, no matter
how big, inconvenient, strange, or scary. You deserve it all.

Seal your desires by dripping red candle wax onto the page and
imprinting it with your thumb, knowing that as you do, you "seal"
the magnetic attraction of all that you desire towards you.

OTHER RITUAL IDEAS

- Create a playlist of songs that remind you of red and dance to inspire courage.

- Create your own passion-filled spells for increased sexual attraction.

- Dress like Kate Bush in the "Wuthering Heights" video and go scare some men.

Orange

"Dance the orange."

RAINER MARIA RILKE

USES IN MAGIC
Enthusiasm, vitality, ambition, creativity, energy, opportunity

IN AN AURA
Adventurousness, independence, inspiration, optimism, health

PLANET
Jupiter

ZODIAC
Sagittarius

DAY OF THE WEEK
Thursday

CHAKRA
Svadhishthana (meaning "dwelling place of the self")

TAROT CARD
Wheel of Fortune, Temperance

CRYSTALS
Carnelian, orange calcite, peach aventurine

HERBS
Damiana, yarrow, calendula

FOODS
Carrots, sweet potatoes, oranges, walnuts, peaches, mangoes, turmeric, almonds

HEALING QUALITIES
Rheumatism, spleen function, appetite, soothes cramps

PSYCHOLOGICAL ASSOCIATIONS
Energy, excitement, playfulness, warmth, creativity, extroversion, independence, dynamism

The use of orange dyes, gathered from natural plants like safflower, marigold, and saffron, is ancient. In South and South East Asia, saffron was the source of dye for centuries. Hindu, Sikh, and Buddhist practitioners have long revered saffron-dyed orange for its associations with sacrifice, renunciation or holiness.

Because of its loudness, orange is often tied up with urgency, celebration, and nationalism. The saffron-orange present on India's national flag stands for strength and courageousness, while *oranjegekte* (orange craze) takes over The Netherlands during major celebrations and sporting events. In Ireland, the orange is associated with Protestantism and features on the country's flag alongside green (for Catholicism) and white (for peace between both groups).

Kandinsky wrote that "orange is like a man, convinced of his own powers," and indeed the color is loud and proud. It's the easiest color to see in low light, making it a popular choice for life rafts, buoys, and road safety signs. Today, orange in the West is considered slightly garish or Bacchanalian, being associated with Halloween and children's advertising.

Because of its cultural meanings, orange is one of the most divisive colors. Many people carry an anti-orange bias without even realizing it. But give it a chance, and orange will revitalize and delight you.

ORANGE AT HOME

Orange exists on a spectrum; from bright tangerines to subdued peach tones. Like all colors, the more intense the shade, the more you can guarantee a strong psychological effect. Softer hues in the home can evoke a feeling of groundedness (think: orangey browns like terracotta) but more commonly, decorating with orange is an intentional act of amplifying one's sense of spunk, stamina, or creativity. In rainbow magic, orange stands for fun, spirited friskiness, and playfulness. Orange is a spell for taking things less seriously.

Use it in work spaces and creative zones to spark an inspired flow and an enthusiasm for getting the job done. Try using orange stationary, sticky notes, or add a motivating orange wallpaper to your computer or smartphone to keep you awake and enthused. Adding orange accents in the bedroom promotes warmth and satisfaction. Find a new piece of art for your walls, like an orange-rich art print. Very '70s.

In the kitchen, the magic of orange shines. Use it to instantly boost your hunger or morning energy levels by adding a thrifted orange cookie jar or storage tins. And if you're a citrus fan, display your oranges in a bowl like the work of art they are. Give their skins a lil' pinch when you're in need of a quick rejuvenating face mist. The energy of orange is a vibrant one. Utilize it in your living space and watch how much more of a knack you have for easeful entertaining.

ORANGE IN CLOTHING + BEAUTY

Orange is one of the best colors you can wear to come across as approachable. It encourages the people you interact with to view you as friendly *and* fun and it helps you to believe the same thing about yourself. It's a social lubricant, a mood lightener and—whether you're the wearer or the observer—it makes people feel good. Consider it your own personal neon sign that states, "I'm here to have fun."

If you're a little shy or awkward and prone to nail biting or thumb-twiddling, wear a citrine ring and look down at it when you need a confidence boost. Want to feel like the life of the party? Slip on an orange outfit and take note of your reflection often. Wearing orange nail polish, shoes, or accessories on a date is a strong but subtle way of presenting yourself as independent and energizing to be around. And if you'd like to work on feeling more inspired, wear an orange artist's apron while doing your creative work. When you need some extra zest, just look down and breathe the color in deeply. Refreshing!

ORANGE AT WORK

A workplace isn't exactly what most of us think of when we hear the word "playful". But thanks to a little orange magic, it can be. Used with intention, bringing splashes of orange to an office creates an air of excitement. Adventure, even. As an easy-going color that's known to increase sociability, add some orange office supplies to your desk or tack an orange picture, like a beautiful sunset, to your wall to bring a sense of ease and fun to your day. Your colleagues might start acting a little more friendly towards you too.

Decorating a workplace with orange can also help with productivity and alertness. If you're in a position to, add more orange to common areas to keep your team upbeat. Just be mindful in your use of this color. Like red, an excess of orange at work could be over-stimulating.

RITUAL: ALTAR EGO

Making an orange-heavy altar to imbue oneself with
encouragement, creativity, and play is the perfect ritual
for anyone looking to live a more inspired and exciting life.

An altar is a space, built just for you, by you. Make them
for specific goals such as personal growth or to encourage
yourself to take on a certain mindset and behavior. Altars
can be tiny and transportable or as big as a dining table. What
they all have in common is this: they're a creative space that
you consider to be sacred.

First, decide on the specific intention for your altar. I
recommend creating a "commitment statement" that you can
remember easily, recite often, and use to help you guide your
decisions. For example, "I commit to living my most enthusiastic,
adventurous life in big and small ways everyday." Once you've
written down your unique statement, choose a quiet space
to build your altar. It could be on the floor in the corner of your
bedroom, on a shelf, or even in a shoebox. The spiritual realm
doesn't discriminate.

Once you've picked your sacred space and cleansed it, it's time
to collect stuff to decorate it with. In the spirit of tidying
expert and Shintoist Marie Kondo, collect things that spark joy.
Orange objects (like candles) that inspire your enthusiasm,
photographs or images, statues or figurines, trinkets or toys,
flowers or herbs, feathers or leaves, art supplies or finished
works, and crystals or tarot cards. Remember, there's *nothing*
that's not altar-worthy. If it reminds you of encouragement,
creativity, or play—if it makes you smile or lights you up
inside—then it's usable.

Now, arrange your most inspiring and encouraging objects on your altar, intuitively. Let yourself place things wherever they seem comfy, not necessarily in the most aesthetic configuration. You can make a ritual of this part by playing your favorite enlivening song and repeating your commitment statement. Keep going until you feel complete.

Try lighting your candle/s and journaling on the floor in front of your altar. You might like to start your day by taking some mindful breaths and repeating your statement, or just gaze at it when you need some extra pep. As you become more comfortable with your altar, more ideas will come to you. If the spirit of orange could talk, it would say: just improvise, experiment, and have fun.

OTHER RITUAL IDEAS

- Use orange crayons or collage to illustrate your magical higher creative self.

- Try open-eye meditation using an orange image or object for encouragement.

- Mindfully eat an orange and describe its qualities out loud while embodying them.

Yellow

"How lovely yellow is!
It stands for the Sun."

VINCENT VAN GOGH

USES IN MAGIC
Intellect, learning, joy, confidence, communication, knowledge

USES IN MAGIC (GOLD)
Inner strength, achievement, blessings, triumph, worth

IN AN AURA
Curiosity, happiness, sharp mind, charm, versatility

PLANET
Sun

ZODIAC
Leo, Gemini

DAY OF THE WEEK
Sunday

ELEMENT
Air

DIRECTION
East

CHAKRA
Manipura (meaning "dwelling place of jewels or gems")

TAROT CARD
The Sun, The Lovers

CRYSTALS
Amber, sun stone, yellow jasper, pyrite, topaz

HERBS
Lemongrass, chamomile

FOODS
Pineapples, cumin, lemons, corn, butter, oats, cinnamon, bananas

HEALING QUALITIES
Memory, stimulates muscles and bile, indigestion

PSYCHOLOGICAL ASSOCIATIONS
Optimism, individuality, hopefulness, self-esteem, transgression, cowardice, positivity, uplifting, savvy

Yellow is a divisive color because it's the strongest, psychologically speaking. Yellow triggers an immediate emotional response, affecting the nervous system more than any other color. It generates energy. Whether we consider that energy positive or negative is up to us. That said, the positive magical qualities of yellow are many.

In the West, the color largely stands for happiness but also, sometimes, cowardice. In China, the color is allied to the Yellow Emperor, Huangdi, a deity slash historical figure. In 19th century Europe, particularly France, yellow also stood for pornographic literature. Hence the scandal of 1895 when British author Oscar Wilde was arrested with a yellow book under his arm.

Yellow is also associated with mental illness, from "yellow house" used in Russian to describe an asylum, to the classic story *The Yellow Wallpaper* by Charlotte Perkins Gilman, which describes a woman's descent into psychosis, to the work of Vincent Van Gogh, whose use of yellow paint increased as his mental health declined, perhaps from lead poisoning from the very same paint.

The joy and elation that yellow triggers persists cross-culturally. As does the timeless awe of its cousin, gold. From alchemists' efforts to places of worship worldwide, gold inspires and stupefies onlookers. And because yellow is the color most resembling gold, it is often used synonymously in art. As art historian B. N. Goswamy wrote, yellow is a "rich luminous color that holds things together, lifts the spirit and raises visions."

YELLOW AT HOME

Color psychologists tend to agree that yellow should be used in moderation at home, because of its strong effect on people's nervous systems and the fact that it's fatiguing to the eye in large amounts. Some even believe that in yellow-painted rooms, people can lose their temper and babies tend to cry more. But when it comes to rainbow power, you are your *own* authority. So the question is: how does yellow make *you* feel? Only experimentation will give you a clear answer. Knowing how you *want* to feel and behave is your anchor in this process.

Yellow also stimulates the mind. And because it's the color of intellectual acumen, its freshness will keep your brain alert and full of ideas when it's displayed around the house. If you're keen to bring a dose of curiosity, smarts, and even mischievousness to your everyday life (especially if you work from home), invest in a bright yellow rug or thrift a tablecloth for your desk. If waking up lighthearted and optimistic is important to you, use a yellow pillow cover or quilt in soft, buttery tones.

If you're looking to feel more awake and get things done quickly, place yellow objects in places you'd like to pay more attention, for example, a yellow umbrella by the door or key chain on your house keys so you don't lose them. Yellow improves your memory, and the eye can't help but notice it. Yellow flowers, ceramics, or purely decorative additions to the home are a magical way to elevate your intellect, stimulate discussion, and boost gladness.

YELLOW IN CLOTHING + BEAUTY

Want to feel like you're walking on sunshine on the daily? Throw on some yellow mules, sneakers, or Docs with yellow laces to get a heart-warming burst of energy everytime you gaze down. Clothes featuring yellow will give you a positive outlook, help you communicate more effortlessly and assert yourself, and it looks great. But be warned, strangers *will* see you as more approachable.

Of course, wearing gold is a strong reminder (for yourself and other people) of your personal power, your worth, and your value. If you can't afford the real thing, gold plated has the exact same effect. No matter your marital status, procuring yourself a ring is a beautiful symbol of self-devotion, deservingness, and your inevitable triumph.

Overall, yellow is a potent form of glamor magic (illusory spells that highlight or conceal something visually) in fashion. It attracts attention and noticeably cheers people up—giving the wearer an instant air of confidence, positivity, and immense intelligence.

YELLOW AT WORK

The thing about yellow, in rainbow magic, is that it's so diverse. Nowhere is this more obvious than in a work environment. Like red and orange, warning signs are often painted yellow, because our eyes can't *not* see it. When it comes to workwear, this can be a double-edged sword; your colleagues may smile when you walk into a room in yellow, but they may also instinctively get more frustrated in conversations with you. Of course, in both cases that's *their* business. For you, the perks are plenty; added focus, lateral thinking, clear communication, and bright ideas.

Having a yellow stapler, smiley face sticker, or stress ball at your desk will help you stay chipper. A bunch of yellow flowers like daffodils, even more so. In common areas, yellow is your go-to color to brighten darkened or boring offices. And design psychology specialist, Karen Haller, recommends it for decorating communal breakfast areas, "if you wish to create a sunny, happy way to start the day." If you're looking to sweeten up a boss or smooth things over with a coworker, add yellow elements to your workspace, clothing, emails (hello, emoji), and anywhere else you want to give off a friendly, welcoming, and open energy. You'll win them over in no time.

RITUAL: COLOR STALKING

Color stalking is usually called 'color walking' and is said to have started as a training exercise for private investigators to increase focus. But the goal isn't focus alone. It's also to cultivate a greater sense of curiosity, optimism, and joy in daily life.

Start by breathing . Then recall or journal all the qualities of yellow that you'd like to magically call into your life right now. State your intention to be emotionally uplifted and reminded of your intelligence, your happy memories, your communication needs, and your hope, every time you see a yellow object. For example, "Everytime I perceive something yellow, I grow more capable, confident, and grateful for the moments of joy all around me."

Now, it's time to set out on foot! If you're not able to go for a walk (because of weather, your age, disability, illness, or safety concerns) do the ritual at home, over as many days as you like.

Start the stalk by noticing something yellow around you. Inhale the joy that this omen is offering to you. Feel the hope and buoyancy of yellow cover you, like an invisible aura. Intuitively decide which direction to go in and keep walking until you see the next yellow object. Keep walking, stalking yellow as you do. Every time you see the color, stop, breathe, and let it make you happy. If it's hard to feel happy, do the polite thing by yellow and just imagine what it would feel like. Once your stalking ritual feels complete, thank whatever invisible or spiritual force you believe in for instilling you with a little more optimism.

OTHER RITUAL IDEAS

- Bask in the sun—for short, safe increments—and soak up its deeply joyful rays.

- Make a "new year's lemon piggy" (no matter what time of year) by cutting small slits in a lemon for ears, a mouth, adding two cloves for eyes, and toothpicks for its four feet. Slip a small coin in the piggy's mouth and charge it with your intention; to bring success and all the blessings associated with yellow. Keep lemon piggy in your home until his job is done. Then give him a proper compost burial.

Green

*"Green how I want you green.
Green wind. Green branches."*

FREDERICO GARCIA LORCA

USES IN MAGIC
Growth, abundance, fertility, wealth, luck, renewal

IN AN AURA
Health-focused, love of nature, generous, practical

PLANET
Venus

ZODIAC
Taurus

DAY OF THE WEEK
Friday

ELEMENT
Earth

DIRECTION
North in the Northern Hemisphere, South in the Southern Hemisphere

CHAKRA
Anahata (meaning "unstruck")

TAROT CARD
The Hierophant, The Empress

CRYSTALS
Jade, emerald, malachite, amazonite

HERBS
Oregano, holy basil, dill

FOODS
Avocadoes, kale, kiwi fruit, matcha, broccoli, limes, cilantro (coriander), green apples

HEALING QUALITIES
Balances blood pressure, sedating, headaches, immunity

PSYCHOLOGICAL ASSOCIATIONS
New life, trustworthiness, nurture, money, environment, poison, envy, refreshment, kindness, youth

As a cool color, green offers a refuge from the stimulus of red, orange, and yellow. The color is damn relaxing. Perhaps our reptilian brain (in charge of our basic survival needs) recognises it as a place containing water and food. We are animals, after all. Green is the most restful color for the eye to perceive.

A certain green color of porcelain, *mi se* (meaning "mysterious color"), was so admired in Imperial China that only royalty could own it or look upon it. It was only 11 centuries later, in 1987, that green-gray celadon porcelain was publicly displayed. Elsewhere in the ancient world, malachite was used to pigment the green Egyptian eye makeup and the green of Tibetan and Japanese Buddha haloes. The Islamic world too reveres green as a holy color: the color of heaven, or paradise, and that of the Prophet Muhammad's (PBUH) cloak.

In the modern world, green is implicitly associated with poison or sickness. This was a legacy of the 19th century's newly invented pigments: Scheele's green and emerald green (used for wallpaper, house paint, clothing, and more) both contained lethal levels of arsenic which caused mass poisoning and often death in the homes of the then-trendy.

Despite the modern association of green with envy, thanks in large part to lines in Shakespeare's *Merchant of Venice* and *Othello*, its celebration is evergreen ... if you will. In the Western collective unconscious, green is linked to Spring, love, youth, fertility, the natural world, and May Day— otherwise known as the revelrous pagan sabbat of Beltane. And due to the prevalence of US media, green will always be synonymous with greenbacks a.k.a cash money.

GREEN AT HOME

In rainbow magic, green is one of the most restful colors to surround yourself with, especially if you need some help unwinding at the end of the day. Because humans are capable of seeing more variations of green than any other color, playing around with different shades in different rooms of the house is worthwhile. For example, adding aqua-green shades in the bathroom (on towels for instance) will help you feel refreshed and blissful after a shower. While adding rich forest green tones in your kitchen (like house plants!) will increase your sense of equilibrium and inspire you to cook with fresh ingredients.

Muted green tones like sage or olive are a magically relaxing addition to your bedroom too. Or if you'd rather wake up feeling invigorated, try putting lime green things, like a dressing gown, in your immediate view to help you wake up—and actually get out of bed. If you're someone who already feels bored or slow-going, brighter greens will help you stay awake and alert without creating a vibe of stagnation (as the softer hues can do in excess).

GREEN IN CLOTHING + BEAUTY

As a witch, wearing green (especially in the Spring months) is like a spell of growth and renewal; a reminder that, like plants, we're a part of nature. Wearing green outer layers is also the perfect tool for visualizing the abundance and/or wealth that's all around you, covering you like a cloak and amplifying your aura with green. Dark greens and those with a softer hue also have the effect of making the people around you feel incredibly at ease in your presence.

While a lime green beret or cap will attract attention straight to your eyes like a magnet, emerald green eye makeup or nails will give yourself and others a restorative and relaxed impression of a person who is chill to be around.

GREEN AT WORK

Want your workplace to be less toxic and more gentle? Add
more plants to common areas. Add as many as you can get
away with. And if your desk is the only area you have any say
in, get yourself a lush green baby or two, like a mini monstera,
devil's ivy, or philodendron. A green apple displayed on your
desk is a great, cheap substitute.

On a personal level, green will inspire you to feel reassured and
safe. And it will help you give off a relaxed, refreshing vibe in
the eyes of others. Communally speaking, sneaking more green
elements into your office will offer your colleagues more
restorative feelings and add an easy-going energy to the space.
For an already motivated team, a little green magic could keep
them on task while helping to prevent panic, stress, or overwork.

RITUAL: THE MONEY JAR

A classic method of manifestation for witches is creating a spell jar, in this case, to attract money.

Start on a Friday (or a new moon) by cleansing a glass container with a non-plastic lid. Breathe, get into a meditative state, and call to mind your goal as a present statement, for example "I am secure, abundant, and money always finds me." Holding your intention in your mind's eye, write it down (ideally with a green marker) on a small piece of paper four times, folding it towards you. Place the paper in your jar, then place four coins in there.

Intentionally add a small handful of money-attracting herbs like basil, dill, or whatever you're intuitively drawn to. Add some honey if you're so inclined (for a sweet, sweet outcome) and seal the jar. Then melt some wax from the bottom of a small green candle around the edges of the lid to seal it further. Next melt enough wax directly onto the lid to be able to safely affix the candle upright. Check that your candle is sturdily attached, light it, and continue to repeat your intention internally, bringing all the emotions of abundance and a'plenty into your body, heart, and mind.

Let your candle burn all the way down (don't leave it unattended) or until you feel a sense of completion. Once complete, be assured that with intention and thoughtful action, a lil' green is coming to you. If you'd like to make a frequent ritual of it, go for it! It's good to use until there's no more space on the lid due to wax build-up. When your ritual is completely over, remove your ingredients and bury them.

OTHER RITUAL IDEAS

- Look up a traditional Metta Bhavana (or "Loving Kindness") guided meditation online and as you privately meditate, see the pure love flowing from your heart space as a warm green light, sending love to all.

- Fill a green glass or vessel with water (or put green cellophane on top of a clear one) and leave it in the sun. After a couple of hours, take it inside and drink it, visualizing all the rest and renewal it's filling you with, with every sip.

Blue

*"Blue color is everlastingly
appointed by the deity to be
a source of delight."*

JOHN RUSKIN

USES IN MAGIC
Healing, forgiveness, harmony, trust, loyalty

USES IN MAGIC (INDIGO OR DARK BLUE)
Meditation, dignity, intuition, beliefs

IN AN AURA
Visionary, compassionate, wise, a healer, principled

PLANET
Uranus

ZODIAC
Aquarius

ELEMENT
Water

DIRECTION
West

CHAKRA
Vishuddha (meaning "pure")

CHAKRA (INDIGO)
Ajna (meaning "command")

TAROT CARD
The Star, The Fool

CRYSTALS
Aquamarine, larimar, angelite

HERBS
Lemon balm, passionflower, mugwort

FOODS
Blueberries, blue corn, blackberries, damson plums, blue candy, indigo tomatoes

HEALING QUALITIES
Soothes nervous system, inflammation, insomnia, phobia

PSYCHOLOGICAL ASSOCIATIONS
Tranquility, calm, introspection, prayer, relaxation, sadness, introspection, sky + sea, sincerity

Whether it's in the form of bright sky-blue or mysterious dark indigo, blue is a color of invocation and the sacred. In the West blue represents heaven and the veneration of the Virgin Mary. Indeed, the history of the Catholic Church is steeped in the centuries-long adoration of that coveted pigment made of lapis lazuli, ultramarine, its translation hinting at its mostly Afghan origin, "beyond the seas".

Blue is often seen as a source of calm and quiet. No surprise then, that it's been associated closely with death as well as God and the afterlife. But there is an intuitive quality to blue as well. Being comparatively rare in nature, blue represents an otherworldliness; the power of the unseen and particularly, unseen forces of safety, security, and the sacred. Organizations, businesses, and institutions of authority use blue to convince people of their trustworthiness, stability, and respectability.

Mediterranean, North African, and Middle Eastern people often seek safety from the evil eye: the envious or malevolent glare of another that could cause harm to the watched. To safeguard against it, many people in these cultures wear various deflective charms, most famously blue ones that resemble an eye. Belief in the evil eye is also common in South Asia and using blue glass beads to shield against it is now a strong fixture of Central and South American culture.

BLUE AT HOME

Soothing tones of blue are a calming addition color in the house, especially for over-stimulated people who seek "serenity now!" as *Seinfeld's* Frank Costanza would say. While too much exposure to blue may influence you with a feeling of coldness or melancholy (don't worry, we're talking a *lot* of blue over a long period), finding the right amount for you is all that matters. And the magical benefits speak for themselves: a patient, harmonious, and calmed mind.

Blue in the bathroom (think: loofahs, soaps, and hair products) is highly recommended for water babies and anyone who wants to step out of the shower mentally as well as physically rejuvenated and oceanic. In the kitchen, use blue to calm you down first thing in the morning by using a blue transparent glass or dish towels. Just be aware that blue is a powerful appetite suppressant, so consider keeping it away from your refrigerator and cooking areas. But as always, your intuition knows best. Speaking of which, blue in the bedroom via pajamas, a hair bonnet, or a lampshade (especially in rich dark shades) will make sure you get a glorious, deep sleep.

BLUE IN CLOTHING + BEAUTY

A baby blue cardigan or eye makeup oozes a kind of peppy yet mellow affability that will make you feel more tranquil and the people around you, even more so. While turquoise is slightly more stimulating, darker blues lean toward relaxation, security, and have an almost sedating effect.

Navy blue has such close psychological associations with uniforms and control, your chic navy blazer is best for times when you want to come across as an authority (like a job interview) without the amped-up quality of red. And when you're "in your head" or in need of answers? Throw on your jeans. We tend to forget that even classic indigo-colored denim is a form of glamor magic. The kind that offers you a particular gut feeling. Call it your internal spiritual GPS; your intuition. No wonder jeans are so popular.

BLUE AT WORK

Next time you're at work, look around. Do you see much blue? Chances are the color of honesty and integrity will be over-represented. After all, businesses love showing off their trustworthiness with blue signage, uniforms, and carpet. But what about you? If you're looking to come across as more authentic and honest, blue is your new work bestie. Go for a subdued blue item of clothing for your next important meeting, especially if it's about a promotion.

And if you need to keep your cool throughout the work day (don't we all?) make like an interior designer meets witch and adorn your personal workspace with blue. Try a candle or crystal you've charged with intention, tropical postcards, or those very '90s bright blue water hourglasses. Stare into it when you need an intuitive hit.

RITUAL: WORRY NOT

A komboloi is usually made up of 23 beads and is very often decorated with blue eyes to guard against the evil eye. The beads are used to relax and stress less.

What are you worrying about unnecessarily? What's your prayer? Where can you find more serenity and release past hurt or future apprehension? Only one way to find out. Breathe and sincerely contemplate it. Then make like a Greek pappoús (granddad) and get yourself a komboloi. If you can't find a real one, just bead 23—or any odd number of blue beads—onto a string and tie it in a loop.

The easiest (and loudest) way to use komboloi is to bring your dominant hand side-on, palms facing you and hold it between your index and middle finger, with half the beads laying against your fingers and half dangling behind them. Then holding the beads facing you in place, flip the beads hanging on the outside of your palm over the top of your index finger so they hit the front ones. Flip them again so they dangle from the outside of your hand once more. Repeat!

If you get stuck, go online to see a demo. If it's still too hard, just rub the komboloi in your palm, or flick one bead at a time in a meditative state. It doesn't matter what your specific intention is, as long as you take it seriously. If you're neurodivergent, you don't need me to tell you how cool a stim toy a komboloi is. And ditto if you're looking to quit smoking— blue komboloi are your stress-relieving new best friend.

OTHER RITUAL IDEAS

- Wear an evil eye amulet for protection. Let your own cultural background determine the kind. Wherever your lineage lies, I can guarantee your ancestors wore protective amulets of one kind or another. Allow this object to feel closer to them and to your own zone of equanimity (no matter what other people energetically throw at you).

- Toning is just like singing or chanting, but without words. If you can hum, you can tone. Next time you feel the need to enter a more relaxed state of consciousness and soothe your nervous system, hum away. Feel the vibrations relax your body and mind (thank you, vagus nerve) as you tone.

Purple

"I think it pisses off God if you walk by the color purple in a field somewhere and don't notice it."

ALICE WALKER

USES IN MAGIC
Divination, spiritual wisdom, purpose, psychic ability, dreams

IN AN AURA
Mysticism, eccentricity, sensitivity, naturally magical, connected

PLANET
Neptune

ZODIAC
Pisces

CHAKRA
Sahasrara (meaning "thousand-petalled")

TAROT CARD
The Hanged Man, The Moon

CRYSTALS
Amethyst, purple fluorite, ametrine, kunzite

HERBS
Blue lotus, lavender

FOODS
Eggplant (aubergine), red cabbages, grapes, purple yams, elderberries, star anise, passionfruit

HEALING QUALITIES
Aids hypnotic states, cooling, concussions, burn out

PSYCHOLOGICAL ASSOCIATIONS
Idiosyncratic, royalty, ritual, spirituality, mystery, religion, luxury, strangeness, magic

Thanks to its history in the Western world as an outrageously expensive color worn only by emperors, purple is still largely associated with the out-of-the-ordinary, the singular, and the remarkable. From the stereotype of "purple people" (usually represented as kooky single women obsessed with all things purple), to the regal purple Robe of Estate donned by Queen Elizabeth II at her coronation, purple is the color of the rare and unique individual.

Purple's status as a special color began in the Ancient Phoencian city of Tyre where two varieties of Mediterranean sea snails had their glands squeezed to produce the opulent, if odorous, natural pigment. Producing one gram of the rare hue took 12,000 sea snails. Of imperial rulers decked in purple-dyed robes, Pliny the Elder wrote, "This is the purple for which Roman fasces and axes clear a way. It is the badge of noble youth... it is called to appease the Gods... it shares with gold the glory of triumph. For these reasons we must pardon the mad desire for it."

In the 19th century, a chemical pigment called mauve was created, democratizing purple once and for all. First a trendy color, this lighter shade of purple soon became tacky due to overuse. Thanks to the misogyny of men like fashion designer Neil Munro Roger who called it "menopausal mauve", lighter shades of purple are associated with old ladies and the weird.

Luckily for mystics, magicians, psychics, and witches for whom the color purple holds a strong magical significance, being weird is a compliment.

PURPLE AT HOME

While all colors contain equally magical properties, purple is unparalleled in its ability to connect us to the spiritual realms. For baby witches and adept occultists alike, displaying purple around the house (especially where sacred objects are concerned) will influence your psychic abilities—the ones that blend your intuition with the external spiritual forces that are meaningful to you, such as spirit guides or deities. Naturally- and ethically-sourced purple crystals like amethyst are recommended as decoration that doubles as a divination amplifier.

Purple ceramics and cushions can help connect you to higher spiritual wisdom in a subtle way in living spaces, while in the bedroom purple throws or images above your bed will help you astral travel and dream lucidly, receiving subconscious messages that you can interpret using a purple dream journal kept by your bed. When using divination tools like tarot, try keeping a purple cloth underneath for extra-potent readings.

PURPLE IN CLOTHING + BEAUTY

Having a hard time owning your weird? Wear something purple, like a pendant or ring. Every time you need an extra hit of self-assurance, gaze at it and inhale to call your power back. Better yet, set an intention to go about your day being 100% your unique self and throw on a whole purple outfit. Hell, dye your hair purple. You'll send a message of defiance and quiet confidence to others (purple being the middle point between the courage of red and the calm of blue) and you'll receive all the benefits of a color that opens up your psychic abilities and amplifies your sensitivity to BS. Win-win.

Because of its association with eccentricity, purple is a "f*ck the haters" color that will support your innate right to live colorfully and wholly express your strange and gloriously captivating nature. Go off, purple person! And a pro tip for purple fanatics: balancing purple with natural, earthy shades can help you stay grounded as you connect with the beyond.

PURPLE AT WORK

Because purple is the last color we humans see before the spectrum of light becomes invisible, it's strongly connected to the higher spiritual realms. What does this mean for work? On the downside, too much purple could decrease your focus and make you seem introverted or "off with the fairies". On the plus side, wearing clothes with purple to work or having purple desk accessories will help you make wise decisions, stay in touch with your spiritual values, and help you stay unflappable in the face of stress.

Purple notebooks, pens, and crystals in your workspace will help you retain your sense of autonomy and help you to remember who you are and what you believe in. Look at them, breathe, and remember you're a profoundly spiritual being having a human experience. Not a productivity robot.

RITUAL: OPEN EYE MEDITATION

If you'd like some help connecting to your spiritual self,
this Trātaka meditation ritual is for you.

First, set a present-tense intention, for example "I am guided by my higher self." Find a soothing, minimal image of something purple, ideally book-size or larger. Find a comfortable position on a meditation cushion, floor, or on chair, facing a wall. Stick your image onto the wall, or lean it against the wall at eye level. If you're not too sensitive to light, place a candle (ideally purple) in front of the image.

Light it, breathe naturally, and let your body feel alert yet deeply relaxed. Begin softly gazing at the tip of the flame and slightly *through* it. If you're not using a candle, focus your gaze at a single point of the purple image. Stay focused, blinking only when needed. When you notice your mind has drifted away, gently and compassionately pull your focus back to its single point. Allow the energy of purple to seep into your consciousness. Do this for 9 minutes (or start smaller) and mindfully contemplate or journal what emotions or spiritual insights came up for you.

If you'd like to extend the ritual, do this meditation daily for 21 days and let purple work its profound magic on you. You're welcome to make the customizations you need to feel comfortable and pain free. And remember, there is nothing wrong with a little movement or fidgeting.

OTHER RITUAL IDEAS

- Using purple mixed media, get into a relaxed, trance-like state and create a psychic abstract artwork, playing intuitively with your materials (without self-judgment) until the piece is done. When complete, use your artwork to scry, divining its subconscious meaning or spiritual messages. You're a psychic *and* an artist!

- What does your Queenly, Kingly, or Themly higher spiritual self look like? Only one way to find out: play dress-up to bring out your most royally psychic alter-ego. Borrow purple clothes off your friends and visit the fabric store if you must! Then look in the mirror and let your reflection teach you something about your power as a witch.

Pink

"I saw a pink sun, and when no one believed me I blocked their sun with the soft side of my hand."

KUSHAL PODDAR

USES IN MAGIC
Love, self-compassion, romance,
friendship, devotion, relationships

IN AN AURA
Kindness, sincerity, generosity,
faithfulness, emotional healing

PLANET
Venus

ZODIAC
Libra

DAY OF THE WEEK
Friday

TAROT CARD
The Empress, Justice

CRYSTALS
Rhodonite, rose quartz, morganite

HERBS
Cloves, rose petals, marjoram

FOODS
Beets (beetroot), açai berries,
dragonfruit, guavas, Himalayan salt,
rhubarb, pink apples

HEALING QUALITIES
Regulates mood, softens aggression

PSYCHOLOGICAL ASSOCIATIONS
Femininity, voluptuousness, affection,
caring, frivolity, pleasure, empathy,
tenderness, nurturing

Baker-Miller pink is a Pepto Bismol-like shade made famous in the '70s when a US researcher, Alexander G. Schauss, found it made people less aggressive and physically weaker. With the prejudicial "war on drugs" underway and incarceration rising, holding cells and youth centers started being covered in Baker-Miller pink. Soon it even showed up on the walls of visiting team locker rooms. Pretty effective, for a "girl's color". So effective that the practice was banned in competitive sports. Sadly not so for prisons around the world.

Before World War II pink was "for boys" due to being a diluted form of the then-categorically masculine red. Now, thanks to marketers of children's clothing and toys, girls are assigned pink—the color known to make one feel physically weaker—often to the exclusion of other colors.

But pink is far from a pushover. Powerful women like fashion designer Elsa Schiaparelli and actress Marilyn Monroe made the intense "shocking pink" the color of glittering, defiant self-determination. Hot pink's stereotyping as a color of promiscuity and bimbos can be seen as a patriarchal backlash—economic as well as cultural, given the "pink tax" on women's products (a 13% markup on average) that continues today.

But despite being diminished and degraded, pink radiates love. Sensual love, romantic love, and even platonic love are the essence of pink's captivating magic. Pink cannot be underestimated. Because, as always, love wins.

PINK AT HOME

Don't let the Baker-Miller pink stories scare you; pink might make you physically weaker and calmer, but in your home life, that's usually a good thing. Especially if you're looking to luxuriate and increase your self-care and self-love practice. Pink ornaments, a couch, or coffee table will not only look cute in your house, their energy will imbue you with a greater sense of self-compassion. Add more pink to your bathroom and you'll find you're more encouraged to keep up any pampering. Pink bath bombs, soaps, and scrubs show your skin and body some extra love at a cellular level.

In the bedroom, pink brings the romance whether partnered or not. Opt for baby pink sleepwear to feel loved-up and venusian even in your sleep. And in the kitchen and areas of high-activity, some hot, shocking pink will keep you feeling physically strong, stimulated, feisty, and ready to take anyone on.

PINK IN CLOTHING + BEAUTY

Gender aside, in matters of the heart, wearing pink strikes just the right chords. Soft pinks have a magically romantic, affectionate, gentle quality. Wear baby pink outfits, hair accessories, or plenty of pink blush to make observers feel all gooey inside—and to feel like you're floating on a pink cloud of self-love.

Less dreamy and more (literally) charming, lipstick in shocking pink is a spell for stealing hearts and staying on someone's mind. Hot pink shoes, tops, and bottoms pull eyes and get phone numbers, no matter who you are. But aside from the obvious fanfare, hot pinks spark a flame inside their wearer; their energy is best described as unapologetic, knowing, and astute—all the spiritual wisdom of purple and all the power and authority of red contained in the one color. Wear hot pinks when you want to feel like the most self-loving *and* self-assured version of you. Elle Woods style.

PINK AT WORK

If you're particularly hard on yourself at work, or someone else is being hard on you, you'll want to make use of the energetics of pink. Even if you can't get away with wearing pink to your job, carry a small tumbled piece of rose quartz in your pocket and grab hold of it when you need to give yourself a big mental hug. Better yet, wear a rose quartz bracelet or a ring with a little pink in it. This is now your magical self-love amulet, use it often and with intention.

If you deem your workplace a little uncompassionate, sneakily add some pink elements here and there to pull at the heart strings of your higher-ups. Decorate with an indoor plant with pink leaves or give out pink pen holders or pens. Your coworkers will thank you. Everytime you look at your pink work accessories, use them as a prompt to answer this basic but ever-important question: how is your heart?

RITUAL: LOVE AND LIGHT

Ideally begun on a new moon or Friday, this simple candle magic spell will help you call in more self-love to reach new depths of devotion to your happiness, confidence, and personal fulfillment.

Start by finding a new candle, ideally pink and pillar-shaped. Then, sit in your sacred space. Relax. Journal or meditate on how you want to feel about yourself, and treat yourself. Intentionally, and from a place of self-worth, cleanse your candle and begin to carve your first name into it vertically from top to bottom. On the other side, carve a short intention statement (an anagram if necessary) in the present tense—something that demonstrates your self-love in your own words. For example, "I deeply respect and love myself" or just "I am loved".

Standing your candle on a fire-safe dish, anoint it with oil. Use your intuition to pick an oil (or just use extra virgin), then add a smidge to your thumb. Rub it on your candle from top to bottom, pointing the bottom to you. Sprinkle herbs on or around the candle. Now charge it with your intention while lighting it. Watch the flame in a meditative state, breathing and connecting deeply with your intention in your mind's eye. When you feel complete, snuff it out. Repeat when needed until your candle is fully melted. Bury (or intuitively dispose of) your melted wax.

OTHER RITUAL IDEAS

- The next time you attend your fave yoga studio,
  set an intention to receive the emotional guidance
  or "downloads" from your heart about what's going
  on for you emotionally. Wear pink. Breathe in pink.
  Notice what comes up and journal about it when
  you get home.

- To deepen your relationship towards your inner child
  (and show them love) get into a relaxed state and
  begin to embody the feelings, however fleeting, of
  love and hope you felt as a child. Putting on a song
  you liked back in the day will help. Then begin to write
  yourself a letter, from the perspective of your
  loved-up inner child. What do they need to tell you?
  Take in their words. Then write back.

Brown

"The color brown... is anything but nondescript. It comes in as many hues as there are colors of earth, which is commonly presumed infinite."

BARBARA KINGSOLVER

USES IN MAGIC
Grounding, the body, the
home, stability, animals, family

IN AN AURA
Longevity, down to earth,
cautious, welcoming, secure

PLANET
Mercury

ZODIAC
Virgo

DAY OF THE WEEK
Wednesday

TAROT CARD
The Hermit, The Magician

CRYSTALS
Smokey quartz, petrified
wood, bronzite

HERBS
Oatstraw, valerian root, skullcap

FOODS
Dates, brown rice, tamarind, chocolate,
potatoes, falafel, hazelnuts, coffee

PSYCHOLOGICAL
ASSOCIATIONS
Practicality, conservatism,
cooking, wood, the opaque,
warmth, dirt, animal fur

Like pink, brown is a misfit, left out of the official color spectrum. But in rainbow magic, brown is far from drab. Brown is the ochre of earth; the first paint pigments. Brown is wood forests, the clay of sculpture, the hides of animals used in humans' first clothing, endless varieties of brown skin on friends, family, and ancestors. Brown is body, home, and hearth. Unglamorous to some, but raw, real, and magic. We all know and love brown. Some of us have simply forgotten.

In 15th to early 20th century Europe and the UK, brown pigment was made, heartbreakingly, from the crushed remains of millions of Ancient Egyptian mummies. The practice ended only because of dwindling supply. In a 1964 *TIME* article, London art shop owner C. Roberson said: "We might have a few odd limbs lying around, but not enough to make any more paint. We sold our last complete mummy some years ago for, I think, £3. Perhaps we shouldn't have. We certainly can't get any more."

The story of mummy brown reveals how far the West has strayed from its roots—we see ourselves as *above* the brown of mud and dirt, not of it. As if we didn't come into the world messy. As if all the science and rationalism in the world can save us from mortality. From eventually going back into the brown soil, feeding, and fertilizing it as we decay.

The magic of brown is the magic of getting acquainted with our own body, nourishing it and tending to it, like we tend to our home and loved ones.

BROWN AT HOME

No matter what shade—from rich mahoganies to neutral tans—homes filled with brown offer a sense of security. Whether real or linoleum (the effect is the same), we've all had the experience of walking into a wood-filled kitchen and immediately feeling comforted. Follow that instinct and add more brown to your kitchen by putting your wooden spoons on display, putting unwashed potatoes in a countertop bowl, or decorating shelves with some driftwood.

You'll feel all cozy, safe, and warm in your living space and bedroom if you buy an extra brown pillow or two, go thrifting and add some more antiquey browns, or throw some neutral dried flowers in a vase on your coffee table. But it's not just about bringing more of the outside, inside, in order to feel grounded. Surrounding yourself with more brown will encourage you to think in pragmatic terms—keeping your head screwed on correctly and dealing with what's in front of you from a centered place.

BROWN IN CLOTHING + BEAUTY

When people talk about being "embodied", they mean being in a state where your body and mind work as a holistic organism, grounded in the truest sense. The magic of brown clothing, accessories, and beauty will assist you in getting curious about your body and responding to its needs, releasing tension, feeling more at one with yourself, in the right relationship with others, and reconnected to nature. And there's a shade of brown for everyone. What they all have in common is their earthiness and stabilizing qualities. When you're looking to feel more sturdy and connected to the ground beneath your feet, wear a brown jumpsuit and shoes. If you need an extra dose of reassurance, pop on a brown lipstick (how '90s) or a brown ring.

I won't lie, wearing brown can sometimes be read by others as being boring, conservative, or "beige". The thing is those poor souls don't know that *every* color is magic. Pity their small minds as you soak in all the solid and supportive energy of the color of earth.

BROWN AT WORK

In work settings, brown decor encourages customers, clients, or staff to view the workplace as reliable, protective, and, potentially, full of warmth. There's a reason so many brands opt for beige graphics on social media; it imitates safety and dependability. Wearing shades of brown to work will do the same. As long as they're clean and stain-free, wearing just about anything brown to work will encourage others to view you as someone who's down to earth, yet should be taken seriously.

In your own work life, brown will help you attract the comforting, reassuring energies of the tallest, thickest oak tree. If you're able, on your lunch breaks or vacations, begin to make a ritual of collecting interesting little stones or pieces of wood. Displaying them at work (and gripping them intentionally as needed) will help ground you when you need it most.

RITUAL: PLANTING ROOTS

Need some grounding brown vibes straight from the source?
This ritual will help you get into your body, let go of stress,
and connect with our great mother, planet Earth.

Find an outside area, preferably with a patch of exposed earth
to sit on, barefoot. Call to mind the people of this land. Who
does it belong to? It could be First Nations people. It could
be your own. Breathe and thank these caretakers, ancestors,
and elders stretching across time. Acknowledge their wisdom.
Mourn the violence beset on their knowledge systems and
bodies, and honor their survival.

If you are not in your own ancestral lands, thank them next.
For example, I would thank my ancestral lands in North Africa,
the Mediterranean, those of the Kalderash Romani, the Celtic,
and East Slavic, seeing those land's colors, sounds, and smells
in my mind's eye. If you don't know about your ancestors,
intuitively imagine their faces and places. Your imagination
is a divine portal so, in doing this, you are very much
connecting with them.

Next, lay your palms to the ground (or press your feet flat
on the earth, if you're in a chair) and breathe. With every
mindful inhale, call up the grounding support of the earth
below you. With every exhale, see your worried thoughts
and unwanted energy leave your body and sink down into
the earth to be composted.

Imagine roots extending from the base of your spine, deep
into the earth. See yourself as sturdy, steady, and as
buttressed as a strong figtree—rooted far into the ground and
immovable. Do this until you feel fully supported. Thank the
brown, magical earth for nourishing you and remember that
you are of it, always.

OTHER RITUAL IDEAS

- Go on a nature walk or hike, treading with care and love. And for every step, see or note something supportive you are grateful for. Let each step be like kissing the earth, going as slow as you like.

- In magic, brown is associated with retrieving lost things. Here's an easy spell for finding lost objects: Light a candle (ideally brown) in a fire-safe dish. Hold out your receptive (non-dominant) hand while looking at the candle and breathing in all the qualities of brown. Say a present-tense intention statement out loud. For example, "What is lost is found again." Closing your eyes, visualize holding the lost object in your hand. Feel its weight, see its color and quality. Keeping your hand held out, intuitively scan for any subtle "pulling" sensations that make you want to face a certain direction or walk a certain way. You'll find it soon enough.

Black

*"There's something about black.
You feel hidden away in it."*

GEORGIA O'KEEFFE

USES IN MAGIC
Protection, banishing, transformation, secrets, releasing, uncrossing

IN AN AURA
Shielding, grief, self-protection, rest, mysteriousness, sophistication

PLANET
Pluto

ZODIAC
Scorpio

TAROT CARD
Judgment, Death

CRYSTALS
Black tourmaline, obsidian, black kyanite

HERBS
Black salt, nettle, bay leaf

FOODS
Blackcurrants, black garlic, jamun, black rice, figs, kalamata olives, black lentils

PSYCHOLOGICAL ASSOCIATIONS
Mourning, anonymity, nothingness, night time, fear, absorption, the unknown, death, space

In the collective unconscious, black represents all things in their unmanifest state; that which is shrouded in mystery. Perhaps that explains our fear of what lies within the "pitch black" of night, but also our reverence for the color of things unknown. As an absorber of all light and therefore all color, black is womb-like, safe, and protective.

The ancient practice of lining one's eyes with black kohl is found in South and West Asia, and North African countries like Egypt. Nobles and commoners used kohl to protect from spiritual forces. In Aztec society, obsidian discs were polished into mirrors to use in honor of the God Tezcatlipoca. One such disc was apparently used by John Dee, occultist and advisor to Queen Elizabeth I, as a scrying mirror to look into and call forth spirits—a practice still popular with some witches today.

Gods of death, and the afterlife, are often represented with jet-black qualities. In the Egyptian *Book of the Dead* the scribe Ani writes, "What manner of land is this into which I come? ... it is deep, unfathomable, it is black as the blackest night." In the West, black images are associated with endings, mourning, or a bleak view of life. Think: funerals, goths, and the "black dog" of depression.

But black represents beginnings too. In the Judeo-Christian book of Genesis, all life was created out of the black of nothingness. Black is the primordial soup. Black is pure potential. It may seem scary, thanks to the meanings projected onto it for a few hundred years, but ultimately black is full of possibility.

BLACK AT HOME

Black may be the most multi-purpose color in all of rainbow magic. Energetically, it can make one feel dignified and mysterious, embodying gravitas. Or it can influence a mood of sophistication. Because of its qualities as a light-vacuum, black can also create a feeling of emotional safety and magical protection in the home. Depending on your sensitivity, an excess of black in the home could feel oppressive or lead you to become overly serious. It depends on your relationship with the color. Experiment and find out!

Black accents in common areas of the home will add an air of substance and elegance, encouraging you to "go within" your own mind when seeking inspiration and knowledge. If you'd like to embrace your academic nature more, black desks, chairs and bookshelves will help bring out your inner philosopher and won't pull focus from your work. Black in the bedroom? You'll wake up feeling protected, undistracted, and like a modern classic.

BLACK IN CLOTHING + BEAUTY

The "little black dress" is timeless precisely because of its magical effect: it makes the wearer feel refined, contemporary, and it requires little effort in terms of styling. No matter what, black is exemplar. Wearing an all-black outfit gives you an air of intellectualism and mystery to others, while helping you to take yourself more seriously and embody self-respect. From smokey black eye makeup to wearing black tights or even dying your hair black, wearing the darkest shade of black is a prescription for emotional safety; a security blanket when you need it most (say a first date or a job interview).

As *the* protective color, black is a spiritual repellent for unwanted energy. On a psychological level, it's a color of camouflage. Wear it when you want to blend in, like the background crew in stage productions do. On a spiritual level, the color acts like a "black hole", disintegrating all negative energy. If you like to add some subtle protection to your clothing and accessories, try jewelry made of tourmaline, black thread or ribbon (chokers are excellent), or a scrunchie or hair tie.

BLACK AT WORK

At the workplace, adding elements of black to your wardrobe, desk, or general workplace acts as a protective forcefield. Got a work frenemy giving you a hard time? Put a black mug or pencil holder between you and them and charge it with the intention of absorbing all their negativity. The more black physically present on or around you at work, the more you'll fly under the radar, so don't be afraid to wear a lot if that's your motive.

In a work sense, black only makes you look more professional. Authoritative even. From Steve Jobs to convicted Silicon Valley fraudster Elizabeth Holmes, black turtlenecks in business are big for a reason. Black, like red, also has a whiff of power to it, so aside from acting as an emotional and spiritual shield, it could even help you get a promotion. You're welcome.

RITUAL: PROTECTION SIGIL

Sigils are a magical intention in the form of a pictorial glyph, charged for a specific purpose. In this case, it is protection against harm.

Relax at your altar or sacred space, breathe, and create a pithy intention for protection, for yourself or someone else. For example, "I am safe at all times". Using a black pen, write down your intention. Now, put a line through all the vowels and repeated letters. In the example above, I would be left with "msftlm". Use the lines of these letters to create a symbol, like the example opposite. It can look any way you like and it doesn't have to be pretty.

Gaze softly and with intention at your sigil. Hold your hands over it to raise its energy. Dance or clap if you like. Or masturbate to imbue the sigil with energy. Repeat your intention and visualize the defensive mist of the sigil's magic rising and rippling out in every direction with power and protection.

Complete charging the sigil in any way you feel called to: by burning, burying, hiding it under an object in your house—whatever. If burning it, use a fire-safe dish and thoughtfully dispose of the ashes. Now get on with your life and allow the magic to do its work.

OTHER RITUAL IDEAS

- Gaze into a black crystal (or any reflective black object, like a patent shoe) as a form of divination.

- When you see them, speak nicely to crows or ravens. They'll remember!

- Spend some time researching banishing spells online and if you ever feel the need arise, experiment with making one of your own.

White

"For colors which you wish to be beautiful, always prepare a pure white ground."

LEONARDO DA VINCI

USES IN MAGIC
Cleansing, peace, clarity,
enlightenment, unity, order

IN AN AURA
Purity, beginnings, innocence,
spiritual illumination, newness

PLANET
Moon

ZODIAC
Cancer

TAROT CARD
High Priestess, The Chariot

CRYSTALS
Moonstone, clear quartz, selenite

HERBS
Pine, garden sage, eucalyptus

FOODS
Rice, coconut, mushrooms, cauliflowers,
tofu, chickpeas, onions, turnips

PSYCHOLOGICAL ASSOCIATIONS
Luminescence, ghosts, cleanness,
chastity, holiness, superiority, simplicity

White is a paradox. On one hand it speaks to sanctity, on the other, to the spooky. White is otherworldly. For modern witches, white's slippery sacredness is a good thing: white can act as a blank substitute for any color or intention in spellwork.

White holds universal appeal as a spritually cleansing color. From the Ihram of Islamic pilgrimage to Mecca to "virginal" bridal gowns, white signifies the holy, the clean, and the close to God. In India and China, white is worn for funerals and mourning because it represents the afterlife. But white can also stand for abject fear ("ghostly pale"), or even intense negative emotions like "white hot rage".

It's an unfortunate reality that in the West, white can be used as a dog whistle for white supremacy. Countless buildings of power have been modeled after the white architecture of Ancient Greece, the West's most romanticized civilisation. However, no Ancient Greek buildings nor classical statues were actually pure white. They were painted a myriad of colors, which over time have faded.

Lead-based white has been the cause of many deaths. In 1970s America, low-income housing for Black, Brown, and First Nations people was often painted with lead-based paint. To this day, when the paint peels, those living in these homes inhale it. It's thought 1.2 million children currently have lead poisoning. Lead-based white has also been mass-produced in women's makeup. While modern forms of skin whitening are still popular in some parts of the world, they no longer contain lead. Only cancer-causing carcinogens. How far we've come.

WHITE AT HOME

Let's talk about the magic effect of white in the home. White elements promise a vibration of peace and quiet. They can aid in increasing your clarity and, like black, they encourage a feeling of emotional security. An excess of white can feel a little too sterile or cold, however. Only you know the difference. Try out some warm off-whites in your bedroom to declutter the mind before bed. A sheet set, rug, slippers, or robe will feel comforting and refreshing simultaneously. Of course, bathrooms usually come in shades of brilliant white. If yours doesn't, add some white fluffy towels, soap dispensers, or display shells along with your white products (like cotton swabs) in containers to help yourself feel clean and orderly.

Like black, choosing white decorative elements for your kitchen or living space (lots of white candles are a crowd pleaser) is an easy and utilitarian choice. You won't have to think too much about it and looking at it daily will help you feel cleansed and peaceful if your outside life is a little hectic. And if after a while, you start to feel that hospital-like coldness, just add more color.

WHITE IN CLOTHING + BEAUTY

It's no wonder Kundalini yogis and other spiritual practitioners wear all-white; it allows a clarity of thought that's unique to this color. Outfits with plenty of white also look consistently aspirational. Likely because they're impossible to keep clean for everyone but the rich. The energy of white will help you feel organized and emotionally neutral from the inside out, in moments where your adrenaline might otherwise spike. Clean white socks, white sunglasses, a pearl necklace, or a white baseball hat are accessible ways to lean into the spiritual potency of white, without having to worry about stains.

Ironically, wearing white can sometimes encourage others to see you as harsh or unapproachable, but in cases where connection is craved, it's nothing your winning personality can't fix.

WHITE AT WORK

You probably don't need me to tell you that an excess of white in work or public spaces can sometimes carry an air of elitism or sterility. In hospitals, the color that represents cleanliness, order, and peace in rainbow magic may be warranted, but in an office? Kinda boring. Focus on the positives by gazing at a blank white space on the wall when you need to calm down or think clearly without influence.

Put some crisp white sticky notes on your desk to encourage an internal sense of order and neutrality in the face of stress. Or better yet, put white stationary objects on your desk, or wear white when you want to send a message of peace and goodwill to the team.

RITUAL: BATH TIME

Performing a bathing ritual is a practice done around the world. Rituals for cleansing oneself are the perfect way to harness the cathartic, purgative power of white to get rid of unwanted energy.

First, start with a clear intention. Breathe and prepare for your bath. If you don't have an actual tub, borrow a friend's or improvise in the shower with a bucket. Just as good! Set the mood with your most relaxing music (or healing nature sounds) and light some white candles.

Begin to draw the bath to your desired temperature (not too hot) and add some or all of: a white bath bomb, some plant-based milk (or dairy milk), epsom salts or natural salts, a cleansing herb picked intuitively, and white flower petals intuitively chosen. Feel free to add anything else that feels cleansing to you such as cleansing lotions or essential oils. If using a bucket, you would simply scoop the mixture onto your body and thoughtfully massage.

If you're in an actual bath, get in and close your eyes. Scan your body. Visualize all the negative energy in your body and mind slipping out and into the cleansing bath. Let the rejuvenating, purifying energy of your white bath seep into you, body and soul. Feel how cleansed you're becoming. Do this until you feel complete. Then get out of the bath and remove the plug, watching all the energetic debris pour down the drain and out of your life. You're all cleansed!

OTHER RITUAL IDEAS

- Look up the practice of *la limpia* or "the cleanse", originating predominantly in Mexico. Online or in person, find a *curandera* (a healer) or *botanica* (spiritual goods store) to instruct you in the ritual, in which you reverently roll a cleansed egg over your body from top to bottom, ridding you of yucky energy. Afterward, you can crack the egg into a bowl of water and read it for divination purposes. Always throw your egg down the toilet or into a running stream afterward.

- Not so much a ritual as an omen to look out for, my Grandmother always said: if in a dream a deceased relative visits you wearing white, it's a gentle and loving warning that something adverse may soon potentially take place. Don't stress. Just be diligent and discerning in your decision-making to avoid unnecessary issues or pain. Kinda like during Mercury retrograde.

Gray

"Gray is the color ... the most important of all ... absent of opinion, nothing, neither/nor."

GERHARD RICHTER

USES IN MAGIC
Balance, decision making,
detachment, impasses, composure

USES IN MAGIC (SILVER)
Warding off, reflection, the
cosmos, shielding, clairvoyance

IN AN AURA
Nervousness, potential, imagination,
sensitivity, astral projection

PLANET
Saturn

ZODIAC
Capricorn

TAROT CARD
The World, The Devil

CRYSTALS
Shungite, hematite, magnesite

HERBS
Rhodiola, hyssop, maca

FOODS
Salted plums, black sesame ice-cream,
charleston melons, oysters, gray salt

PSYCHOLOGICAL ASSOCIATIONS
Doubt, neutrality, objectivity,
indecision, bad weather, nuance,
bargaining, sadness, versatility

From brutalist urban landscapes to shining precious metal, gray and her sparkly counterpart silver are both exalted and taken for granted. Gray is the color of nuance. It appears in angst-ridden movie scenes as clouds, concrete, or ambiguous wastelands. A gunmetal polish or sparkly silver sheen speaks to the future: rocket ships or chrome-covered robots.

Like the Tin Man from *The Wizard of Oz*, gray things can be read as unemotional or even heartless. And it's kinda true; gray's magic contains an objectivity. It is diplomatically placed at the exact intersection of black and white. Its energy contains the protective, transformative essence of black and white's power to purify, making it a potent color of assurance and peace.

Gray sees all sides to every argument, balancing heated emotion and taking the best course of action for the most people with the most sustainable results. Gray is the impartial negotiator of rainbow magic. Whatever your goals, gray will amplify them with dedicated neutrality.

Now imagine those qualities of protection and purification came in a glossy, reflective coating. You're thinking of silver, the color of shields, silver bullets, the silver branches used to enter the fairy world in Scottish folklore. Associated with Goddesses and the moon, silver aids in cultivating a second sight—contact with the unseen and the clairvoyant ability to view the future. Silver is what we see when we look up at night to view a sky of infinite twinkling stars. Precious is an understatement.

GRAY AT HOME

Whether in shiny tones or matte, gray in rainbow magic can act as a gateway to the unconscious and invisible world of spirit. That means for witches-in-training, there's no better color to help with astral travel or connecting to different dimensions, if that's your thing. Gray or silver candles, silver-toned crystals, and other shiny things on your altar or in your living spaces can help your experimentations along. While gray has a reputation for reminding people of old age and emotional dullness, adding it to your bedroom, bathroom, or kitchen can assist in balancing your mood and opening your mind to new possibilities and potentials.

In terms of sending any negative energy back to where it came from, add a mirror in a perpendicular position to your front door or else place a bagua mirror outside the home, ideally after consulting with a feng shui practitioner on how to do this considerately. Overall, gray elements will help you stay composed, quiet your inner monologue, gain broader perspectives and detach from worrying about the outside world. An excess of gray however, can potentially feel gloomy or cause confusion. As ever, you know best. And if you don't, experiment.

GRAY IN CLOTHING + BEAUTY

Gray is the color of pure neutrality in rainbow magic. Wear when you want to give off completely unbiased vibes. Gray is so inoffensive to others, it's almost a smoke screen on which people see what they want to see. That makes it a perfect job interview color if your potential employers are looking for even-handed flexibility, or first date color if you want to embody an air of being cool and slightly aloof. When it comes to how the magic of gray will make you feel, expect equilibrium—self-assurity and a serene disposition. Wear a chic and cozy gray sweater or trousers to help feel poised and stable on otherwise wobbly days. And if you want to remain immune to the influence or potential manipulation of others, throw on gray underwear under your clothes and wear all your favorite pieces of sterling silver.

And speaking of silver, metallic gray eye makeup, hair accessories, or even piercings adds a stealth imperviousness to the would-be energy vampires, while at the same time, helping you to connect to spirit or source. Whatever that means for you.

GRAY AT WORK

In office politics, gray allows you to be Switzerland; spared from the drama going on around you. If you'd like to fly under the radar on the job, wearing elements of gray or carrying around gray objects (a binder, your phone case, or a KeepCup) will help you hide so you can get on with it. Of course, many traditional offices, warehouses, and even retail stores are already gray-walled. Make the most of it by focusing on something gray around you when you need to balance yourself out on a feelings level. This color can promote healthy forms of "zoning out" temporarily, daydreaming, or emotional restoration.

Thanks to silver's connection with the moon, rather than emotional restoration it may incite a little emotional amplification at certain times of the moon's cycle. But with that deep feeling comes the chance to peer beyond the veil of everyday reality, however briefly. Wear silver to work, carry a silver water bottle, or display silvery stationary or decorative items on your work desk to keep your spiritual practice (especially your extrasensory perception and kinship with celestial transits) close to you.

RITUAL: ROAD OPENER

In rainbow magic, gray frees up impasses and deadlocks, removing obstacles by opening up situations. If you're at a standstill or stuck between a rock and a hard place, this spell is for you.

In its equitable, big picture wisdom, sometimes gray knows best. Use this ritual to open up the road in front you, but proceed with respect for the things out of your control. There may be a long game that's playing out.

First, sit at an altar that includes gray things or in a sacred space, relax, breathe, and connect with your center. This can be your body's center of gravity, just above the belly button, or anywhere physically that feels central to you. Set your heart on creating an intention statement relating to freeing up a gridlock. It could be general, for example, "I free the road in front of me from obstacles". Once your intention is solid, proceed.

Take a small candle (ideally gray) and place it on a fire-safe dish. You're welcome to dress the candle by anointing it in oil such as abre camino oil, a road-opening herbal oil found through Afro-Caribbean suppliers. Light the candle. Write out your intention statement on a small piece of paper (ideally gray) and place it underneath your candle. On four new pieces of paper, draw arrows. Position these around your candle with the arrows pointing out.

Hover your hands over the candle flame and hold your intention in your mind to energetically charge your spell. If it feels powerful for you, repeat your intention aloud. When you feel complete, state "the path is cleared" if it feels good to do so. Snuff out your candle (if it's not already dissipated) and dispose of your remaining wax—ideally at a road's intersection.

OTHER RITUAL IDEAS

- Use a silver gel pen to keep a grimoire or journal of your cosmic experiences.

- Put holographic or metallic silver stickers on your stuff to keep adversaries away.

- Free-write on gray paper as a form of catharsis and acceptance of the unknown.

- Imagine a silver bubble shielding and protecting your whole body as a practice in energetic boundaries.

Fear No Colors

"My heart leaps up when I behold
A rainbow in the sky: So was it when my
life began; So is it now I am a man;
So be it when I shall grow old,
Or let me die!"

WILLIAM WORDSWORTH

When we connect to the magic of color, we connect to our true selves; liberated in self-love, generously and intuitively expressive, confidently creative, and resiliently joyful. Not only does cultivating a close relationship with color help transform our emotional lives and influence the way we behave in the world for the better, but appreciating color is a gateway to gratefully appreciating all of life. To looking at the world through new eyes. To manifesting your wildest dreams. To living colorfully.

In rainbow magic, you now have a powerful framework for understanding your individual psychology and your spirituality in playful new ways. I've said it before and I'll say it again; the version of rainbow magic presented here is not about rules. Use this book as the inspiration you need to make your witchcraft, your creativity, or daily expression uniquely your own. I guarantee you that experimenting with your *own* rainbow power will not only be fun, it'll be fruitful. It will bring you to brighter, richer levels of self-worth, spiritual growth, and personal fulfillment.

Because that's what the magic of color is all about. Enjoying the whole spectrum of human emotion. Relishing in every tone and shade of experience. Reclaiming your power. Standing in full saturation. And painting your world rainbow.

May you always live colorfully.

Table of Correspondences

	Planet	Zodiac Sign	Day of the Week	Element
Red	Mars	Aries	Tuesday	Fire
Orange	Jupiter	Sagittarius	Thursday	
Yellow	The Sun	Leo Gemini	Sunday	Air
Green	Venus	Taurus	Friday	Earth
Blue	Uranus	Aquarius		Water
Purple	Neptune	Pisces		
Pink	Venus	Libra	Friday	
Brown	Mercury	Virgo	Wednesday	
Black	Pluto	Scorpio	Tuesday	
White	The Moon	Cancer	Monday	
Gray	Saturn	Capricorn	Saturday	

Direction	Tarot	Chakra	Crystals	Herbs
South in N.Hemisphere, North in S.Hemisphere	The Emperor The Tower	Muladhara	Garnet Red jasper Ruby	Dandelion root Ginger Ashwagandha
	Wheel of Fortune Temperance	Svadhisthana	Carnelian Orange calcite Peach aventurine	Damiana Yarrow Calendula
East	The Sun The Lovers	Manipura	Amber Yellow jasper Pyrite	Lemongrass Chamomile
North in N. Hemisphere, South in S. Hemisphere	The Hierophant The Empress	Anahata	Jade Emerald Malachite	Oregano Holy basil Dill
West	The Star The Fool	Vishuddha Ajna	Aquamarine Larimar Angelite	Lemonbalm Passionflower Mugwort
	The Hanged Man The Moon	Sahasrara	Amethyst Purple fluorite Kunzite	Lavender Blue lotus
	The Empress Justice		Rhodonite Rose quartz Morganite	Rose petals Clover Marjoram
	The Hermit The Magician		Smokey quartz Petrified wood Bronzite	Oatstraw Valerian root Skullcap
	Judgment Death		Black tourmaline Obsidian Black kyanite	Black salt Nettle Bay leaf
	The High Priestess, The Chariot		Moonstone Clear quartz Selenite	Pine Garden sage Eucalyptus
	The Devil The World		Shungite Hematite Magnesite	Rhodiola Hyssop Maca

References

Adler, M. (2006)
Drawing Down the Moon : Witches, Druids, goddess-worshippers, and other pagans in America.
Penguin Books

Agrippa, C. (2021)
Three Books of Occult Philosophy.
Inner Traditions

Ashby, M. and Vijaya Ashby, K. (2005)
The Egyptian Book of the Dead.
Semi Institute Of Yoga

Ashby, N. (2018)
Color Therapy Plain & Simple: The only book you'll ever need.
Hampton Roads Pub

Batchelor, D. (2013)
Chromophobia.
Reaktion

Blavatsky, H.P. (2014)
The Secret Doctrine: The synthesis of science, religion, and philosophy.
Theosophical University Press

Buckland, R. (2010)
Buckland's Practical Color Magick.
Pendraig

Cameron, J. (2016)
The Artist's way: 25th anniversary edition.
Penguin Books

Campbell, J. (1949)
The Hero With a Thousand Faces: A brilliant examination, through ancient hero myths, of man's eternal struggle for identity.
Fontana Press

Carroll, P.J. (1992)
Liber Kaos.
Welser

Chang, T.S. (2018)
Tarot Correspondences.
Llewellyn

Crowley, A. (2021)
Four Books of Magick: Liber ABA.
Random House

Eason, C. (2018)
A Little Bit of Auras: An introduction to energy fields.
Sterling Ethos

Éliphas Lévi. (2011)
The History of Magic.
Lost Library

Lanier Graham, F. (1979)
The Rainbow Book.
Vintage Books

Birren, F. (1984)
Color: A Survey in Words and Pictures: From ancient mysticism to modern science.
Citadel Press

Birren, F. (2013)
Color Psychology and Color Therapy:
A factual study of the influence of
color on human life.
Martino Publishing

De Angeles, L. (2016)
Witchcraft: Theory and practice.
Llewellyn

Fenton-Smith, P. (2008)
The Tarot Revealed.
Allen & Unwin

Finlay, V. (2009)
Colour: Travels through the paintbox.
Sceptre

Goethe, V. (1970)
Theory of Colors.
M.I.T. Press

Goswamy, B.N. (1986)
Essence of Indian Art.
Asian Art Museum Of San Francisco

Haller, K. (2019)
The Little Book of Colour:
How to use the psychology
of colour to transform your life.
Penguin Life

Horowitz, M. (2020)
Magician of the Beautiful:
An introduction to Neville Goddard.
Gildan Media

Jill Badonsky. (2010)
The Nine Modern Day Muses
(and a Bodyguard).
Renegade Muses Publishing House

Johari, H. (2000)
Chakras:
Energy centers of transformation.
Destiny Books

Judith, A. (1996)
Eastern Body Western Mind:
Psychology and the chakra
system as a path to the self.
Celestial Arts

Jung, C.G. (2013)
Man and His Symbols.
Stellar Classics

Kandinsky, W. (2006)
Concerning the Spiritual in Art.
Tate

Leadbeater, C.W. (2008)
The Inner Life.
New Age Books

Leathers, H and Campkin, D. (2011)
The Advanced Workbook For
Spiritual & Psychic Development.
Spreading The Magic

References

Parma, G. Meredith, J. (2018)
Elements of Magic:
Reclaiming earth, air, fire,
water, and spirit.
Llewellyn

Perkins Gilman, C. (2003)
The Yellow Wallpaper.
Rain City Projects

Plotinus (2019)
The Enneads.
Cambridge University Press

Sark (2001)
Eat Mangoes Naked:
Finding pleasure everywhere
and dancing with the pits!
Simon & Schuster

St Clair, K. (2018)
The Secret Lives of Colour.
John Murray Publishers

Vaneigem, R. (2001)
The Revolution of Everyday Life.
Rebel Press

Von Hagen, C. (1971)
401 Party and Holiday
Ideas From Alcoa.
Golden Press

Waite, A.E. (1973b)
Pictorial Key to the Tarot:
In full color.
Causeway Books

Walker, A. (1982)
The Color Purple.
Weidenfeld & Nicolson

Wen, B. (2015)
Holistic Tarot.
North Atlantic Books

Willis, P. (2013)
Colour Healing Manual:
The complete colour
therapy programme.
Singing Dragon

Wilson, C. House, R. (1971)
The Occult: A History.
Random House

Acknowledgments

This book was written on sovereign, unceded Gadigal and Bidjigal country. I acknowledge and send my solemn respect to the Indigenous elders of this land, past, present, and future.

My deep thanks to the following people: Kajal Mistry, Satu Hämeenaho-Fox, and the wider Hardie Grant team; the fabulous Coleen O'Shea; and the talented Han Valentine. A sincere thank you also to the cute and colorful Ariel Katz and Babka; my inspiring friends and family; and the generous mentors and peers who uplift me. Finally, thank you to my clients for their willingness and trust. Your curiosity, drive, magic, and creativity inspire me everyday.

This book is dedicated to the closeted creatives, witch-curious, would-be writers, neuro-outlaws, chaos agents, bad artists, weird dressers, queer dreamers, shy romantics, dogged survivors, joyful freaks, recovering perfectionists, the rule breakers, and everyone defiantly expressing themselves, or longing to.

About the Author

Jerico Mandybur (they/she) is a neurodivergent author, award-winning creativity coach, tarot reader, and meditation teacher. With an accomplished background in writing, editing, content strategy, and podcasting, Jerico helps creatives to unlock their unique intuitive expression and live a more mindful, magical life. Jerico's work and words have appeared everywhere from *New York Magazine, Vogue, LA Times, New York Times, The Guardian, Refinery29*, and many more. Their favorite color is black.

JERICOMANDYBUR.COM

Previous releases by Jerico Mandybur: *Neo Tarot: A fresh approach to self-care, healing and empowerment, Daily Oracle: Seek answers from your higher self,* and *Pleasure Oracle: A love, sex and pleasure deck.*

Published in 2022 by Hardie Grant Books,
an imprint of Hardie Grant Publishing

Hardie Grant Books (London)
5th & 6th Floors
52–54 Southwark Street
London SE1 1UN

Hardie Grant Books (Melbourne)
Building 1, 658 Church Street
Richmond, Victoria 3121

hardiegrantbooks.com

British Library Cataloguing-in-Publication Data. A catalogue record
for this book is available from the British Library.

Rainbow Power
ISBN: 978-1-78488-566-3

10 9 8 7 6 5 4 3 2 1

Publishing Director: Kajal Mistry
Acting Publishing Director: Emma Hopkin
Project Editor: Satu Hämeenaho-Fox
Design and Art Direction: Hannah Valentine
Illustrations: Hannah Valentine
Production Controller: Nikolaus Ginelli

Colour reproduction by p2d
Printed and bound in China by Leo Paper Products Ltd.